R 12.1

D1326942

12 S

27·1·90

INTERNATIONAL COPYRIGHT LAW AND THE PUBLISHER IN THE REIGN OF QUEEN VICTORIA

answered by the pressure round his neck of a pair of arms, in shrunken sleeves, which were perfectly capable of an effusive young foreign squeeze.

"Dreadfully ill — I don't see it!" the young man cried. And then, to Morgan: "Why on earth didn't you relieve me? Why didn't you answer my letter?"

Mrs. Moreen declared that when she wrote he was very bad, and Pemberton learned at the same time from the

illustrations — letters that he was divided between the impulse to show his present disciple, as a kind of wasted incentive, and the sense of something in them that was profanable by publicity. The opulent youth went up, in due course, and failed to pass; but it seemed to add to the presumption that brilliancy was not expected of him all at once that his parents, condoning the lapse, which they good-naturedly treated as little as possible

but how could Morgan live on him? What was to become of him anyhow? Somehow, the fact that he was a big boy now, with better prospects of health, made the question of his future more difficult. So long as he was frail the consideration that he inspired seemed enough of an answer to it. But at the bottom of Pemberton's heart was the recognition of his probably being strong enough to live and not strong enough to thrive. He him-

of furniture. Pemberton's spirits were low, and it came over him that the fortune of the Moreens was now even lower. A blast of desolation, a prophecy of disaster and disgrace, seemed to draw through the comfortless hall. Mr. Moreen and Ulick were in the Piazza, looking out for something, strolling drearily, in mackintoshes, under the arcades; but still, in spite of mackintoshes, unmistakable men of the world. Paula and Amy were

The Lesson of the Master 1892
(See pp. xii and 81)

INTERNATIONAL COPYRIGHT LAW AND THE PUBLISHER IN THE REIGN OF QUEEN VICTORIA

BY

SIMON NOWELL-SMITH

James P. R. Lyell Reader in Bibliography
Oxford University 1965-1966

OXFORD
AT THE CLARENDON PRESS
1968

Oxford University Press, Ely House, London W. 1

GLASGOW NEW YORK TORONTO MELBOURNE WELLINGTON
CAPE TOWN SALISBURY IBADAN NAIROBI LUSAKA ADDIS ABABA
BOMBAY CALCUTTA MADRAS KARACHI LAHORE DACCA
KUALA LUMPUR HONG KONG TOKYO

PRINTED IN GREAT BRITAIN

TO THE MEMORY OF
MICHAEL SADLEIR
AND
LARS HANSON

PREFACE

The invitation to give the James P. R. Lyell lectures in 1965–6 came as a flattering surprise. With no training in bibliography or research and little experience of lecturing I was minded to refuse. A miscellaneous book collector, a bibliographically undisciplined snapper-up of uncoordinated and often trifling facts—*multiplex est sciolismus at transibit*—could hardly hope to sustain a theme through five evenings before a critical academic audience. However, a chance encounter in Sanders's Bookshop in the Oxford High Street led to a theme. My eye was caught by an old friend, George Meredith's *The Amazing Marriage*, with an unfamiliar face, a binding with the imprint of a publisher whom I had not associated with Meredith. Many years earlier I had puzzled over other editions of this book with Michael Sadleir: now I was spurred to renew my excursion in Victorian bibliography by Lars Hanson, keeper of printed books in Bodley and one of the Lyell electors. The pursuit led to further problems of British publishing history and to international law, and it was these that I decided to explore. It was matter of the deepest regret that the second of my two mentors should have died, suddenly and before his time, a bare fortnight before the first lecture was given.

Written for speaking to a domestic Oxford audience the lectures are now printed almost exactly as they were spoken. The conversational tone and the digressions must be excused. What I attempted was not a contribution to scholarship so much as a cursory survey of a field in which some areas had not yet been thoroughly excavated. If the survey should stimulate further research, whether my findings are confirmed or controverted, something will have been gained. A few passages omitted in delivery for lack of time have been restored. The discussion of *The Amazing Marriage* has been shortened because a fuller account has been published elsewhere.

The material in the lectures is selective, as it must be when so large a subject is treated in so brief a compass. On the publishing side the selection has been largely from records I have happened upon in the course of unrelated studies: archives of other publishers might lead to quite other conclusions. On the legal side judgments have been quoted to illustrate particular points: other judgments equally or more important in settling or unsettling the law have been ignored. Many of the assertions concerning the laws of various countries are simplifications, and some may be over-simplifications. It has not seemed necessary when using the word 'author' to explain that frequently, as one statute puts it, it 'includes any person claiming through an author'—that is, the copyright proprietor be he publisher or other assign; and I hope that the uses of the word 'book' are not so loose that the different meanings are in context ambiguous. Historians of copyright vary in their choice of dates for certain international agreements. I have tried to be consistent in, for instance, attributing the Anglo-French convention to 1852 and the Berne convention to 1887, the years when they were ratified, rather than 1851 and 1885–6 when they were first negotiated.

The period covered is the reign of Queen Victoria, 1837–1901, with inevitably some discussion of what had gone before. Though the narrative sometimes spills over into the twentieth century I have deliberately not dealt with the considerable changes embodied in the United States copyright act of 1909 and the United Kingdom copyright act of 1911. To have done so would have required at least two more lectures.

I would express gratitude first to the electors to the Lyell readership and secondly to my wife. For help of various kinds—access to documents and permission to quote from them, loan of books, information, criticism, advice—my debts are many, more particularly to the delegates of the Clarendon Press; to the publishing houses of George Bell, William Heinemann, Macmillan. John Murray and Bernhard Tauchnitz; to Messrs. T. & A. Constable, printers, and Messrs. John Dickinson & Company, paper-makers; to Australia House Bookshop (London); to the following libraries or individual members of their staffs—the Bodleian, British Museum, London Library, National Library of Scotland, St. Bride

Printing Library, Auckland Institute and Museum, Alexander
Turnbull Library, Honnold Library, Pierpont Morgan Library and
the libraries of the universities of Melbourne, Harvard, Texas and
Yale; to Professor James J. Barnes, Dr. Jacob Blanck, Mr. Donald
G. Brien, Mr. Harry Carter, Professor C. L. Cline, Dr. Esmond
S. de Beer, Professor Leon Edel, Professor Gordon S. Haight, Pro-
fessor O. Kahn-Freund, Mrs. J. R. H. Moorman, Mr. Percy H.
Muir, Mr. Vivian Ridler, Professor Joseph Rykwert, Mrs. Charles
Sadler, Mrs. Kay Soper and Professor Kathleen Tillotson.

S. N.-S.

Headington Quarry, 1966

CONTENTS

LIST OF ILLUSTRATIONS

Acknowledgments are due to the Bodleian Library for figs. 7, 8*a*, 10 and 11; to the British Museum for fig. 8*b*; and to the Tauchnitz Verlag for fig. 9. The other illustrations are from the author's copies. The frontispiece half-tones are from photographs by Thomas-Photos, Oxford.

I

INTRODUCTORY: EMPHASIS ON
THE PUBLISHER

THE subject of these lectures is the effect of national copyright laws and international copyright conventions upon publishing and printing practices between 1837 and 1901. They will be concerned with the publication of British books in Europe, in the United States and in the British dominions and colonies. There will be something to say also about the publication of foreign books, particularly American books, in Britain. In some of its aspects this subject is familiar to all students of nineteenth-century literature; in some it has been covered by all writers of text-books on the laws of copyright. I shall try to avoid as far as possible the most familiar aspect of all, the public discussions and recriminations which preceded every change in the law. We all know that authors who felt themselves defrauded of a divine right to the rewards of their profession—Wordsworth and Carlyle and Washington Irving, Dickens and Wilkie Collins and Charles Reade—inveighed against what they regarded as the thieving, piratical activities of foreign publishers of their works. We know that one of the chief aims of the Society of Authors, founded in 1884, was to promote national legislation and international treaties to secure to authors the benefits they claimed. And we know or could easily find out what the publishers both of copyright editions and of piratical editions thought of their rights and their rivals; what obstacles the lawyers envisaged in seeking to redress real or fancied wrongs; and how legislators introduced into the discussions questions of morality and expediency, of public enlightenment and the public purse.

I say we could easily find out these things. They are there to be read in the memoirs of authors and publishers; in the files of newspapers and trade journals; in *Hansard* and in the reports of royal commissions. In fact though they are vaguely familiar to many of us they have never been very thoroughly explored. Professor James J. Barnes, of Wabash College, Indiana, recently embarked upon a full-scale study of Anglo-American copyright in the nineteenth century and I am unwilling to anticipate his findings, the more so because of his generosity in exchanging ideas with me—a somewhat one-sided process as anyone who has encountered Professor Barnes's well-stored memory will appreciate. I propose therefore to concentrate less on legislators and societies of authors than on publishers; less on disputation before some change in the law than on the practical effects of the law when passed, effects sometimes very different from what the legislators intended.

I am not a lawyer; and even if I were I might find it impossible to answer some of the questions I shall pose. Some are questions to which bibliographers so far as I know have not devoted much thought. But the answers are part of the stuff of publishing history which is itself a branch of bibliography. And since I was led to pose certain questions by puzzlement over the oddities of one late-Victorian novel I propose to plunge straight into the 1890s and to attack the problem that led me to my theme before starting a review of the law, as any well-mannered lecturer would do, with Queen Anne. Queen Anne after all is dead and can lie quiet for another quarter of an hour. By taking George Meredith's *The Amazing Marriage* as a lawyer might say 'out of time', and at the risk as Coleridge would have said of 'hystero-proterizing'—that is, translated for the benefit of the unlearned, putting the cart before the horse—I shall endeavour to explain how I arrived at the belief that the practical effects of copyright legislation could be as important to a publisher on the production and distribution sides of his business as they were to an author who, having written his book, hoped to reap financial profit from it.

In the Bodleian, undifferentiated in the catalogue except by pressmark, there are two copies of *The Amazing Marriage*, Westminster, Archibald Constable & Co., two volumes, 1895. One was deposited in 1896 under the copyright law and the other came many years later with the Hugh Walpole bequest. They have so far as the eye can detect identical title-pages with identical printer's imprint on the versos. But in Copy A (Walpole e. 470, 1) each title-leaf is integral to its half-sheet, whereas in Copy B (256. e. 9735, 6) these leaves are cancels. In Copy A the text of Volume I ends at the foot of p. 269 (R7 *recto*) with the pregnant last sentence of Chapter XXIV—'He could not conceal that he was behind the door' (fig. 1). In Copy B four lines of text have been carried over to p. 270 (R7 *verso*). The collation of both volumes of Copy A is straightforward,† Volume II beginning with new pagination and a new series of signatures (fig. 3): Volume II of Copy B, how-ever, runs on its pagination and signatures from Volume I, the first leaf of text being a singleton signed R* (fig. 4). The first text page of this volume contains 21 lines in Copy A and 23 lines in Copy B. The imposition, including the number of lines to the page and involving some resetting, varies as between the two copies throughout the last half-dozen pages of Volume I and the first dozen of Volume II: moreover, as can be seen in the contents lists in figs. 3 and 4, all the rectos of Volume II from sig. B onwards of Copy A appear as versos in Copy B, and *vice versa*. (I should perhaps say at this point that there are no author's textual revisions to account for these changes.) Another marked difference is that Copy A is printed throughout on a rough-surfaced antique wove paper and Copy B on a similarly rough imitation-laid paper. I shall return to the clue of the imitation-laid paper.

Why the resetting? the altered pagination, imposition, and sig-natures? the different paper? More than twenty years ago Michael Sadleir at my request sought a solution from the printers, T. & A. Constable of Edinburgh, but their reply was inconclusive and we gave up the mystery as insoluble. Stored for a quarter of a century in that lumber-room which does duty for the mind of a miscel-laneous collector these mysteries suddenly surfaced when I saw in an Oxford bookshop in 1965 a copy of *The Amazing Marriage*

---

† *Copy A.* Vol. I: π^4 A–R^8; pp. viii, 269, 270 imprint, 271–2 blank. Vol. II: π^4 A–R^8 S^4 T^2; pp. 1–2 blank, vi, 282, 283–4 blank. *Copy B.* Vol. I: π^4 ($\perp\pi$2) A–Q^8 R^8 (–R8); pp. viii, 270. Vol. II: $2\pi^4$ ($\perp 2\pi$3) R*^{1} S–2L^8 2M^4; pp. 1–2 blank, vi, 271–551, 552 blank.

closed book of the binding, to this raw philosopher, or he would not so coldly have judged the young wife, anxious on her husband's account, that they might escape another scorching. He carried away his impression.

Livia listened to a remark on his want of manners.

'Russett puts it to the credit of his honesty,' she said. 'Honesty is everything with us at present. The man has made his honesty an excellent speculation. He puts a piece on zero and the bank hands him a sackful. We may think we have won him to serve us, up comes his honesty. That's how we have Lady Arpington mixed in it—too long a tale. But be guided by me ; condescend a little.'

'My dear ! my whole mind is upon that unhappy girl. It would break Chillon's heart.'

Livia pished. 'There are letters we read before we crack the seal. She is out of that ditch, and it suits Russett that she should be. He's not often so patient. A woman foot to foot against his will—I see him throwing high stakes. Tyrants are brutal ; and really she provokes him enough. You needn't be alarmed about the treatment she'll meet. He won't let her beat him, be sure.'

Neither Livia nor Gower wondered at the clearing of the mystery, before it went to swell the scandal. A young nobleman of ready power, quick temper, few scruples, and a taxed forbearance, was not likely to stand thwarted and goaded—and by a woman. Lord Fleetwood acted his part, inscrutable as the blank of a locked door. He could not conceal that he was behind the door.

FIG. 1. Volume I, end of Chapter XXIV, copy A

stand thwarted and goaded—and by a woman.   Lord
Fleetwood acted his part, inscrutable as the blank of
a locked door.   He could not conceal that he was
behind the door.

CHAPTER XXV

THE PHILOSOPHER MAN OF ACTION

GOWER's bedroom window looked over the shrubs of
the square, and as his form of revolt from a city life
was to be up and out with the sparrows in the early
flutter of morning, for a stretch of the legs where
grass was green and trees were not enclosed, he rarely
saw a figure below when he stood dressing.   Now there
appeared a petticoated one stationary against the rails,
with her face lifted.   She fronted the house, and while
he speculated abstractedly, recognition rushed on him.
He was down and across the roadway at leaps.

'It 's Madge here!'

The girl panted for her voice.

Mr. Woodseer, I 'm glad ; I thought I should have
to wait hours.   She 's safe.'

' Where ? '

' Will you come, sir ? '

' Step ahead.'

Madge set forth to north of the square.

He judged of the well-favoured girl that she could
steer her way through cities : mouth and brows were a
warning to challenger pirate craft of a vessel carrying

FIG. 2. One-volume, Chapters XXIV–XXV

THE AMAZING MARRIAGE

CHAPTER XXV

THE PHILOSOPHER MAN OF ACTION

GOWER's bedroom window looked over the shrubs of the square, and as his form of revolt from a city life was to be up and out with the sparrows in the early flutter of morning, for a stretch of the legs where grass was green and trees were not enclosed, he rarely saw a figure below when he stood dressing. Now there appeared a petticoated one stationary against the rails, with her face lifted. She fronted the house, and while he speculated abstractedly, recognition rushed on him. He was down and across the roadway at leaps.

'It 's Madge here!'

The girl panted for her voice.

'Mr. Woodseer, I 'm glad ; I thought I should have to wait hours. She 's safe.'

'Where?'

'Will you come, sir ?'

'Step ahead.'

Madge set forth to north of the square.

He judged of the well-favoured girl that she could steer her way through cities : mouth and brows were a warning to challenger pirate craft of a vessel carrying

VOL. II.   A

FIG. 3. Volume II, pp. vi and [1], copy A

THE AMAZING MARRIAGE

CHAPTER XXV

THE PHILOSOPHER MAN OF ACTION

GOWER's bedroom window looked over the shrubs of the square, and as his form of revolt from a city life was to be up and out with the sparrows in the early flutter of morning, for a stretch of the legs where grass was green and trees were not enclosed, he rarely saw a figure below when he stood dressing. Now there appeared a petticoated one stationary against the rails, with her face lifted. She fronted the house, and while he speculated abstractedly, recognition rushed on him. He was down and across the roadway at leaps.

'It's Madge here!'

The girl panted for her voice.

'Mr. Woodseer, I'm glad; I thought I should have to wait hours. She's safe.'

'Where?'

'Will you come, sir?'

'Step ahead.'

Madge set forth to north of the square.

He judged of the well-favoured girl that she could steer her way through cities: mouth and brows were a warning to challenger pirate craft of a vessel carrying guns; and the red lips kept their firm line when they yielded to the pressure for speech.

K*

FIG. 4. Volume II, pp. vi and [271], copy B

published not by Archibald Constable in Westminster but by George Bell & Sons in London and Bombay. It was a single volume dated 1895, a year (actually six months) earlier than the first cheap one-volume Westminster edition dated 1896 (fig. 5). It was printed on a smooth wove paper, whereas the Westminster single volume is on rough imitation-laid paper; and the verso of the half-title bore the legend 'This Edition is issued for Circulation in India and the Colonies only'. All the mysteries were at once clear. In case any of you do not immediately see the solutions, I will confess that I did not feel wholly happy about my own deductions until I had visited Edinburgh and, with the courteous help of the printers, had examined the contemporary records. I have also been provided by Texas University Library with, among other revealing documents, a copy of Meredith's contract with Constable's of Westminster for the domestic and colonial editions of *The Amazing Marriage*.

To cut a long story short,† Constable's of Westminster had ordered from Constable's of Edinburgh in the autumn of 1895 three printings: 2,000 copies in two volumes on best antique wove; 2,500 copies in one volume on a cheaper wove, with Bell's imprint, for simultaneous publication in the colonies; 4,500 copies dated 1896, on imitation-laid paper, for the one-volume cheap edition to be published in the following spring. All three editions or impressions were machined in October 1895, the two-decker and the colonial were published in November and the cheap Westminster edition went into storage.

For the change from two volumes to one certain changes of imposition were necessary. Volume I of Copy A, as we have seen, ended at the foot of a recto. The text of Volume II naturally began under a drop-head on another recto. To close what would otherwise have been an unsightly gap Chapter XXIV with Lord Fleetwood

† For a fuller discussion of the complexities of this book see my article 'The Printing of George Meredith's *The Amazing Marriage*' in the *Library*, December 1966. A point not made there, though of some interest, is that the impression printed for Bell's (following the text of Copy A) can be shewn to have been printed before the one-volume domestic impression (which gave birth to Copy B); in the former Lord Fleetwood is described on page 286 as going to 'matins at a Papist chapel', but in the latter, as in all subsequent printings, he goes to 'mass'.

still unconcealed behind the door was coaxed over to page 270, and Chapter XXV was made to follow on (fig. 2). Continuity of pagination involved some over-running for several pages on either side of the gap, leading to the reversal of rectos and versos for the latter part of the volume. The signatures were also altered to make a single series.†

There the story might have ended. It is a common enough pattern. But an unforeseen demand from the circulating libraries meant that the publishers would need another 500 copies as soon as possible in two volumes. That in turn meant changing back to two-volume imposition. In order to save time they instructed the printers to take 500 sheets of the stored domestic one-volume edition, sigs. A–Q and T–2M, to provide appropriate prelims, and to reprint sigs. R and S as cancels with, again, the necessary amount of over-running and reimposition. Hence the mysterious Copy B, on imitation-laid paper, with sig. R divided between the two volumes.

It may be asked what this narrative, which obviously concerns publisher and printer, has to do with international copyright. The connection lies in the words 'colonial edition' and in the deduction that, had no colonial *Amazing Marriage* been required simultaneously with the two-decker in November 1895, there would have been none of this pother: the two-decker imposition would have remained undisturbed until nearer the time for printing the domestic cheap edition in the following May. Colonial editions were designed to combat cheap foreign—mainly American—editions piratically imported into the colonies. International copyright conventions were designed to defeat piracy, and acts of parliament defined the conditions and limits of copyright in the British colonies. When I had cut my way through the tulgey wood of the problems of *The Amazing Marriage* I came out on to a landscape of colonial publishing almost wholly unexplored by bibliographers.

Colonial editions according to Mr. John Carter's *A.B.C.* are 'regarded by collectors with disfavour'. Henry James's bibliographers, Professors Edel and Laurence, justifying their summary

† One-volume collation. a^4 b^2 A–2L^8 2M^4; pp. xii, 551 [552 blank].

THE AMAZING MARRIAGE

BY

GEORGE MEREDITH

AUTHOR OF 'THE ORDEAL OF RICHARD FEVEREL,'
'THE EGOIST,' 'DIANA OF THE CROSSWAYS,'
'RHODA FLEMING,' ETC. ETC.

LONDON
GEORGE BELL AND SONS
AND BOMBAY
1895

FIG. 5a. Colonial title-page

THE AMAZING MARRIAGE

BY

GEORGE MEREDITH

WESTMINSTER
ARCHIBALD CONSTABLE AND CO.
1896

FIG. 5b. Domestic title-page

Macmillan's Colonial Library

THE TRAGIC MUSE

BY

HENRY JAMES

London
MACMILLAN AND CO.
AND NEW YORK
1890

No. 109 *The Right of Translation and Reproduction is Reserved*

Fig. 6a. Colonial title-page

THE TRAGIC MUSE

BY

HENRY JAMES

London
MACMILLAN AND CO.
AND NEW YORK
1891

The Right of Translation and Reproduction is Reserved

Fig. 6b. Domestic title-page

treatment of such editions say that they have 'only a relative bibliographical importance', which is only true if you hold that there
can be relative importance on the publishing-history side, as there
certainly is on the collecting side, of bibliography. They say also
that it was standard procedure for British publishers to issue a
colonial edition simultaneously with the domestic one-volume
edition, and that to their knowledge no Henry James colonial
edition contained new material or textual revision. The first statement is not quite accurate. As we have seen, the colonial *Amazing
Marriage* was published several months before its domestic counter-
part; so was at least one of James's novels, *The Tragic Muse*. 'The
colonial edition of this', wrote Macmillan's anxiously to their
printers in June 1890, 'should be published within a week of the
English'—that is the English three-decker—'but as you have not
yet begun the working of it we hardly see how this can be done.'
Collectors with an eye to priorities should surely look with greater
favour on a colonial *Tragic Muse* dated 1890—it was published in
August—than on the domestic one-volume edition dated 1891,
published in February (fig. 6). James's bibliographers give more
than half a page to full bibliographical treatment of the domestic
edition as against a single line to the colonial, which incidentally
they misdate. So much, for the present, for *The Amazing Marriage*
and the colonies.

It is customary for British lecturers on international copyright
to begin not with the 1890s but with Queen Anne, and to assert
proudly that the first copyright act passed anywhere in the world
was 8 Anne, c. 19 (1709), and that the world's first *international*
copyright act was that to which Queen Victoria's assent was given
in the first year of her reign (1 & 2 Vict. c. 59). The assertions are
fair enough even though Queen Anne had never met the word
'copyright'—nor would she have found it, had she lived so long,
in Dr. Johnson's *Dictionary*†—and even though the statute of the
young Queen Victoria in 1838‡ nowhere mentions 'international

---

† The earliest example of 'copyright' in *O.E.D.* is dated 1767, but the word appears
(as 'copy-right') in the Encouragement of learning bill, H.L.R.O., parchment coll.,
H.L. 6 May 1735.   ‡ For the Prussian law of 1837 see p. 41 below.

copyright'. So far as I have observed, the phrase 'international copyright' first reached the statute book in 1844 when another act (7 & 8 Vict. c. 12), repealing that of 1838, designated it 'for the sake of perspicuity' the 'International Copyright Act'. As for British pride in priority of legislation—pride, they say, comes before a fall. The trouble caused by Queen Anne's act for more than a century is outside my subject, though you will hear echoes of it. Through the series of copyright enactments to which Victoria moving into middle age gave her assent a whole caravanserai of coaches-and-horses could have been, and indeed may be said to have been, driven. In 1878 her Majesty's trusty and well-beloved commissioners, having inquired into 'the laws and regulations relating to home, colonial and international copyright', included in their report the following paragraphs:

> The first observation which a study of the existing law suggests is that its form, as distinguished from its substance, seems to us bad. The law is wholly destitute of any sort of arrangement, incomplete, often obscure, and even when it is intelligible upon long study, it is in many parts so ill-expressed that no one who does not give such study to it can expect to understand it. . . .
>
> The fourteen Acts of Parliament which deal with the subject were passed at different times between 1735 and 1875. They were drawn in different styles, and some are so drawn as to be hardly intelligible. Obscurity of style, however, is only one of the defects of these Acts. Their arrangement is often worse than their style. Of this the Copyright Act of 1842 is a conspicuous instance.

The act of 1842 (5 & 6 Vict. c. 45), later known for the sake of perspicuity as the 'Copyright Amendment Act', or the 'Imperial Copyright Act', or more familiarly 'Talfourd's act', was not fully repealed for sixty-nine years.

We are committed to exploring the relationship between the law and the publisher. If the commissioners' strictures were just, if an ordinary hardworking business man whose day was taken up with authors, manuscripts, printers, proofs, binders, booksellers, not to mention rivals and pirates, could only be expected after long study to find the law hardly intelligible, then we can only say 'Pity the poor publisher'. Part of my thesis is the perplexity of the poor publisher. Of course instead of the conflicting statutes he could consult legal text-books. Legal text-books tend to be revised at intervals of ten or more years, often after some major change in the law. But the law seldom stands still, and publishing never. Take for example Copinger, a name still venerated among biblio-graphers—*Copinger on Copyright*, first edition 1870, second edition 1881, the second no doubt aided to some extent by the clarifications of the royal commission. If Copinger can be assumed to be reliable for 1870 and 1881, what about the intervening years? If a publisher relied on the edition of 1870 did he regulate his relations with authors and printers and oversea distributors for a decade without considering the effects of case law before the next edition, or the next statute? Was he aware of the implications for copyright of a subsection in an act concerning customs and excise or merchandise marks, or of a judicial interpretation of a phrase in an act concern-ing patents? Were his contracts with authors still valid, or did they need revision, when a new act was passed? Were they invalidated by the terms of an injunction in the court of chancery, or a judg-ment in the court of Queen's bench or common pleas, or on a writ of error in the exchequer chamber, or in the House of Lords? Did he keep abreast of the legislation and the legal decisions of other countries? Did he even, perhaps knowingly, ignore the provisions which his own legislature had devised for his own protection? Would he have been happy even to define terms like 'international copyright' and 'piracy'? Can *we* define them?

As I must use these terms I shall essay definitions, or perhaps rather anti-definitions.

First, international copyright. I propose to use the expression quite loosely. It has been argued that there can be no such thing as 'international copyright' law; that there are only national copy-right laws and *inter*-national conventions granting more or less reciprocal privileges to subjects or citizens of other nations. This is mere pedantry. Since 1844 when the words 'international copy-right act' found their way into the statute book, more evidently since 1846 when Britain's first international conventions, those with Prussia and Saxony, were signed, and positively since the

Berne convention of 1887, the phrase 'international copyright law' has had usefulness and meaning. Moreover I shall apply it un-ashamedly in that lawless period between Queen Anne and Queen Victoria when nationals of one country or another, authors and publishers alike, were hopelessly seeking to discover what rights they might claim as aliens, beyond frontiers and oceans, in nations not their own.

Secondly there is the term 'piracy'. It can be applied more or less precisely or it can be applied imprecisely. According to a youthful but still invaluable essay by Mr. Graham Pollard, 'as long as the work of a foreign author was not legally protected it was common property; it was no more piratical for a publisher to print it than for a peasant to graze his pigs on common land'. (Though formerly the owner of cow-rights on an Oxfordshire common I am unable to say whether *all* peasants enjoy pig-rights.) Mr. Pollard maintained that 'author's copyright . . . was not speci-fically recognized as personal property in England until 1842, nor by international agreement until 1887'. This—apart from the date 1887 being I think forty years too late—is less than the whole truth. In common law the author's complete and perpetual power over his unpublished writings seems never to have been in serious doubt. 'Copy right' is concerned with published 'copies', and in these the statute of Queen Anne, 'singularly ill-framed to secure the privilege of booksellers'—the phrase is Augustine Birrell's—'did (for the first time) confer upon authors a qualified and time-limited property'.

Before 1842 it was frequently debated in the courts, and variously decided, whether an author had a common law right to his writings after publication or whether such right, if it had ever existed, had been extinguished by Anne's act which granted him a limited statutory right. That the right had been extinguished was decided by the House of Lords in the case of *Donaldson* v. *Becket* in 1774, but that did not prevent lower courts from finding loopholes in the Lords' decision. For as publishing became more complex so problems arose which had not been in the minds of earlier legis-lators and on these the earlier statutes had inevitably been silent.

Where the law is silent, insufficient or obscure it is the practice of the courts to conform to natural law and the rules of equity. Furthermore it was frequently debated, and variously decided, whether in certain circumstances even a foreign author was not entitled to the same legal protection for a qualified and time-limited property as a British subject. A judicial decision in one year might give a legal blessing to a category of publication which would be deemed piratical by the decision of another court a year or two later. However all this may be, I shall use the term 'piracy' if only for convenience in the unrestricted sense in which it was commonly used at the time—that is, meaning any appropriation by a publisher with no substantive right to it of a piece of writing to which its author or his assign claimed a title whether by statute, by natural law or in equity. 'Moral piracy' as Wordsworth called it was a phrase often on the lips of pre-Victorian authors and publishers.

In this matter of anti-definitions you will perhaps have winced at my shocking misuse of the term 'edition' when speaking of the different printings of *The Amazing Marriage*, all basically from the one setting of type. Throughout these lectures when it seems convenient to do so I shall continue to use the term, not as your modern bibliographer does, but in the good, round, uninhibited Victorian way. When a Victorian publisher caused a well-leaded three-decker to be reprinted, still as a three-decker, he put the words 'second edition' on the title-page; when the leads had been removed, the type re-imposed and duplicate or triplicate stereos or electros made, two or perhaps three printers printed as single volumes an 'American edition', a 'colonial edition' and a 'cheap English edition'—perhaps several 'editions' of each. Authors of text-books on the principles of bibliographical description or of A.B.C.'s for collectors must blame the Victorians, not me. After all I have the law at least for my period on my side. In the case of *Reade* v. *Bentley* in 1858—Charles Reade accusing Richard Bentley of printing more 'editions' of *Peg Woffington* and *Christie Johnstone* than Reade had bargained for—it was held

that edition means every quantity of books put forth to the bookselling trade and to the world at one time; and that when the advertisements, the printing, and other well-known expenses and acts by a publisher bringing out such a quantity of copies in the ordinary way, are closed, that constitutes the completion of the edition, whether the copies are taken from fixed or moveable plates or types, and whether all the types or plates are broken up or not, and whether all the copies are given forth and advertised for sale, or retained and stored in the warehouse of the publisher.

As Vice-Chancellor Page put it more succinctly, 'A new "edition" is published whenever, having in his storehouse a certain number of copies, the publisher issues a fresh batch of them to the public.'

To return to Queen Anne. The *raison d'être* of the act of 1709, the justification if it were such for 'Vesting the Copies of Printed Books in the Authors or Purchasers of such Copies', was as expressed in the title 'the Encouragement of Learning'—or as the phrase is expanded in the preamble 'the Encouragement of Learned Men to Compose and Write useful Books'. This pious intention was introduced into the bill beyond doubt to ease its passage. The bill was promoted by publishers—that is, by what were then known as booksellers and are called in the act 'the purchasers of copies'. Their aim was not altruistic: they did not care much about the encouragement of learned men, and assuredly they did not want the copies 'vested' whether in the authors or in themselves for a limited period. Their bill was not for 'vesting': it was, as the title read on first and second readings, for 'securing the property of copies of books to the rightful owners thereof'. This phrase carried the implication that an author or his assign had *ab ante* a rightful property in the work, whereas the amendment in committee, 'vesting the copies of printed books in the authors or purchasers . . . during the times therein mentioned', implied that the authors and publishers had no inherent right of property at any other time. The times therein mentioned were two consecutive periods of fourteen years. The amendment defeated half the purpose of the original promoters. The author seemingly lost his common law right after publication and the publisher his hope of purchasing perpetual copyright. Hence many tears. Hence also much of the uncertainty among authors, publishers and the courts about the rightful ownership of useful books.

C

There was nothing in the act of 1709 to distinguish learned men of foreign allegiance from British subjects. The distinction crops up later with the argument that the British parliament can only have intended to legislate for British subjects. Nor did the act limit copyright protection to books printed in Britain: for years afterwards counsel quoted one of the few acts of the ill-fated Richard III (1 Ric. 3, c. 9) as evidence that even in the cradle age of printing parliament, while determined to protect English craftsmen from the competition of cheap foreign labour at home, nevertheless sought to encourage learning by allowing the import of foreign books. The idea that a book should only be protected if printed in the country where protection was claimed was as irrelevant to English law in the early eighteenth century, and indeed almost always later, as it was basic to United States law from the moment the Americans began to think seriously about international copyright.

American and French copyright law in the nineteenth century have their roots in the revolutions which took place in the eighteenth. In America the story starts with a resolution of the Colonial Congress in 1783, recommending the several states 'to secure to the authors or publishers of any new books . . . being citizens of the United States . . . the copy right of such books' for two periods of fourteen years each (*Journal of Congress*, viii (1783), 256–7). Some of the states adopted or adapted the phrase 'the encouragement of learning'; none of their acts spoke of 'vesting the copies'. In 1790 the first United States Congress passed a public act (*Statutes at Large*, i (1845), 124–6) securing copyright to authors 'being citizens of these United States, or resident therein'. The definition of 'resident' was to give trouble in the years to come, and the word was finally interpreted as limited to a resident who had declared his intention of taking up citizenship. Another section of this act expressly allowed the importation, vending, reprinting and publishing in the states of any book written or published abroad by any person not being a citizen—a quite unnecessary provision, it might be thought, since in any case such books could not obtain copyright. But if unnecessary it was an encouragement to American publishers to reprint popular English books without the author's consent and without remunerating him. In fact the law was designed to benefit United States citizens—authors, publishers and printers—and to penalize the subjects of the kingdom from which the states had successfully revolted. The protectionist policy was not to reach its extreme point until a hundred years later when it was enacted that, in order to secure copyright, a book must be manufactured in the United States (*Statutes at Large*, xxvi (1891), 1106–10).

In the second year of the French Republic in the month of Thermidor the Convention as might be expected abolished the monarchical system of royal licence to print and extended the widest rights to living authors—by implication perhaps at first only to *citoyens*. An imperial decree of 1810, however, specifically mentions as beneficiaries of copyright protection '*les auteurs, soit nationaux, soit étrangers*'.† A French citizen did not have to have his book first published, let alone printed, in France: the mere fact of publication wherever effected established his copyright at home.

Thus it came about that there were three distinct lines of thought converging upon international copyright by the time of Queen Victoria's first international copyright act. There was the English line (the encouragement of learning), the French line (*à tous la liberté*), and the American line ('My country, 'tis of thee . . .'). The three interacted. The British author wanted recognition on the French model for his natural right to his intellectual progeny the world over. The British publisher wanted for the copyrights he had bought a protection which would enable him to compete with the protectionist Americans. Most of the British legislation in Victoria's reign was directed towards reconciling these three points of view. And while the author was most vocal in proclaiming his natural rights and the inadequacy of his financial return from the benefit that the fruit of his labour conferred upon foreign readers and publishers—in fact the iniquity of what he considered foreign piracy—it was upon the British publisher who had sunk

---

† *Loi relative aux droits de propriété des auteurs d'écrits en tout genre*, 19 July 1793; *Décret contenant règlement sur l'imprimerie et la librairie, tit. VI, art. 40*, 5 February 1810.

hard cash in his business of publishing that the double burden fell of combating the pirates and persuading the legislature of the economic as well as the moral insufficiency of the law.

While on this subject of the encouragement of learning and without wishing to go into all the many changes of the law between 1709 and 1837 let me quote one other eighteenth-century act (15 Geo. 3, c. 53) particularly relevant to an Oxford audience, an act of 1775. Queen Anne by limiting copyright to a term of years had abolished 'perpetual copyright', but George III re-established the perpetual copyright of works published by certain places of learning—'the Two Universities in *England*, the Four Universities in *Scotland*, and the several Colleges of *Eton, Westminster,* and *Winchester*'. The profits were to be applied to the advancement of learning and 'other beneficial purposes of education within the said universities and colleges'. Perpetual copyright in Britain might seem to have little to do with international copyright since it could only obtain where the royal writ ran. But the international implications for publishers of this innocent and well-intentioned domestic act extended well into the twentieth century. And having begun my lecture in the late nineteenth century I propose very logically to end it in the twentieth, and to end it in Oxford.

Of Dr. Jowett's lively concern over the United States copyright act of 1891 something will emerge on a later occasion. The Master of Balliol died in 1893 bequeathing his literary property to his college; and Balliol being a part of our university thereby acquired the property under the act of George III in perpetuity. One of the sections of the act reads:

Provided nevertheless, That nothing in this Act shall extend to grant any exclusive Right otherwise than so long as the Books and Copies belonging to the said Universities and Colleges are printed only at their own Printing Presses within the said Universities and Colleges respectively . . . ; and that if any University or College shall delegate, grant, lease, or sell their Copy Rights, or exclusive Rights of printing the Books herein granted, or any Part thereof, or shall allow, permit, or authorize any Person or Persons, or Bodies Corporate, to print or reprint the same, that then the Privileges hereby granted are to become void and of no Effect.

This applies of course only to printing and reprinting in the king's dominions. To secure American copyright Jowett's voluminous *Plato* in its revised edition had to be printed in America. It was entrusted to the New York firm of De Vinne in 1891. In the following year electros were made—3,407 electros weighing two-and-a-half tons.† In 1901 this not inconsiderable weight of metal passed to J. J. Little & Co. of New York who reprinted the work in 1908. Eleven years later the Oxford University Press Inc. of New York asked their printers, now the J. J. Little & Ives Company, to reprint again, only to be told that the two-and-a-half tons of electros in 72 stout boxes had been 'lost'. Here was a pretty problem. We need not go into the litigation which resulted after some years in the award of $5,000 to the Press in New York. Our problem is one of international, and perpetual, copyright. Both the University Press in New York and the Clarendon Press in Oxford wished in 1919 to put out a reprint in America. Short of resetting the whole work in New York what could they do? Oxford-printed sheets imported into America would have been contraband, but in fact there were no Oxford-printed sheets immediately available. To manufacture the book in England by some quick photographic process and export sheets would not only infringe United States law: it would mean employing an outside firm—that is, allowing, permitting and authorizing some person or body corporate in the dominion of George V to reprint the same and thus rendering the perpetual privilege void and of no effect. What the master and fellows of Balliol and the Clarendon Press actually did is not for me to divulge—I do not wish to put their copyright in either country at risk after the delegates have generously given me access to their archives.

† This figure is taken from the Clarendon Press records. The *Publisher's Weekly's* estimate (5 May 1923) was four tons.

II

ENGLISH LAW TO 1852

I WANT next to deal with certain effects upon publishing practices of the laws passed and some of the judicial decisions delivered in the earlier part of Queen Victoria's reign. The chief aspects of British law as it affected international copyright are the status of the foreign author wishing to secure protection in the British dominions, the restrictions imposed on the import of foreign books into those dominions and the measures prescribed to exclude piratical imports. There are also to be considered the measures taken by the publishing trade to combat piracy. The acts of parliament which affected publishers of books are concerned not only with books and encyclopaedias, periodicals and newspapers, but also with musical compositions and dramatic performances, the fine arts and engravings, patents and customs regulations. I shall run briefly through the statutes which dealt in whole or part with international copyright in *books*, and shall then consider some of the judge-made law in the period.

There are five copyright acts and five relevant customs acts in the eighteen years from 1838 to 1855,† and four relevant acts in the eleven years between 1875 and 1886.‡ Taking the earlier group first, the international copyright act of 1838 empowered the Queen by order in council to grant the same privileges of copyright to authors of books published in foreign states as they would have enjoyed if they were British subjects whose books were first pub-

---

† 1 & 2 Vict. c. 59, 1838 (international copyright); 5 & 6 Vict. c. 45, 1842 (copyright amendment); 5 & 6 Vict. c. 47, 1842 (customs); 7 & 8 Vict. c. 12, 1844 (international copyright); 8 & 9 Vict. cc. 84 & 93, 1845 (customs); 10 & 11 Vict. c. 95, 1847 (foreign reprints); 15 & 16 Vict. c. 12, 1852 (convention with France); 16 & 17 Vict. c. 107, 1853 (customs consolidation); 18 & 19 Vict. c. 96, 1855 (customs amendment).

‡ 38 & 39 Vict. c. 12, 1875 (international copyright); 38 & 39 Vict. c. 53, 1875 (Canadian copyright); 39 & 40 Vict. c. 36, 1876 (customs consolidation); 49 & 50 Vict. c. 33, 1886 (international and colonial copyright).

lished in the United Kingdom. It was a condition that the foreign state should grant reciprocal though not necessarily identical privileges to British authors. The act was the outcome of protracted discussions between British, French and Prussian publishers and between the three governments. But whether because no foreign state was willing to play on our terms or, as is more probable, in view of insufficiencies in the drafting of the act, witnessed by the many attempts made in the next six years to amend it, no order in council was signed. The act was abortive and the foreign author had to wait several years before he had any chance of enjoying British copyright by statute.

The copyright amendment act of 1842 was a more general act, designed 'to afford greater Encouragement to the Production of Literary Works of lasting Benefit to the World'. It remained the basis of domestic copyright law until 1911. With its main object, the prolongation of the term of copyright, we are not concerned. More pertinent to our purpose is that the act revised the law relating to the registration of books and the deposit of copies in copyright libraries. Henceforth a copy of every new book seeking protection, and of every later edition with alterations or additions, must be delivered to the British Museum—within one month if the book was published 'within the Bills of Mortality' (which means, it seems, in any London parish); within three months if published elsewhere in the United Kingdom; and within twelve months if published in any other part of the British dominions. In place of registration of all books at Stationers' Hall, which had nominally been compulsory for some 200 years, the act merely made registration a condition precedent if a claimant to copyright wished to pursue his claim in the courts. Delivery to the museum and to other libraries, and registration at the hall, are what may be called domestic provisions of the act; but they become relevant later with the obligation to register protected foreign books.

The international provisions of the act of 1842 deal with penalties, and with the copyright owners' remedies at law, for piracy. No one in the British dominions in effect might print any copyright work without the proprietor's consent; nor might he import a book for sale or hire or sell it if, having been first published and copyright in the United Kingdom, it had been reprinted outside the British dominions. It should be noted here that the act speaks of import 'for sale or hire' and lays no restriction on import by a private person for his personal use. Lord Mahon, one of the sponsors of the bill, had written to John Murray before the act was passed of the hardship which private persons resident abroad would suffer:

> Suppose for example a man of slender means goes abroad for the education of his children; he buys for their use a large assortment of books—Hallam's, Lingard's, Milman's Histories; Southey's or Wordsworth's Poems—all in foreign editions. What is he to do in returning? Is he bound to fling all these literary treasures, enriched perhaps with his pencil marks and annotations, from the packet-deck?

Lord Mahon could safely import literary treasures for two years from 1842 provided that he neither sold nor hired them. The act of 1844 however 'absolutely prohibited' the importation of copyright works printed abroad without the copyright proprietor's written consent.

Section 17 of the 1842 act besides imposing penalties for the importation of piracies authorized the seizure of piratical works by any officer of customs or excise, 'and the same shall be destroyed by such officer'. Section 23 however deemed piratical imports—presumably when they had successfully eluded the customs—the property of the copyright owner who might sue for recovery or for damages. (It is a pleasing thought, if I may be allowed a momentary digression, that later in the century her Majesty's customs found in the Trinity House a better destination for forfeited piracies than the incinerator. As the secretary of customs put it when inviting the connivance of publishers, 'The gift of such books to the libraries of lightships and lighthouses can hardly be detrimental to the sale of the works in the United Kingdom and Commonwealth'.) Later in 1842 advantage was taken of a new customs act to revise the provisions of the main act with regard to piratical books. The new regulations were framed to lighten the burden of the officers and make for greater efficiency in detecting piracies.

Proprietors of copyright if, but only if, they were prepared to take active steps to protect individual publications against piracy were required to supply the customs with particulars of those publications and of the duration of their copyrights. The customs were then required to print lists of the books for public exhibition at all United Kingdom ports. At this stage only, be it remarked, United Kingdom ports. The general prohibition of piracies throughout the oversea dominions under the earlier act remained in force; but this was distinct in the eyes of the law from the narrower obligation of the customs to seize notified titles in the United Kingdom.

As Mr. Gladstone explained in a letter to John Murray soon after the act was passed,† it had seemed a 'fairer and more manageable system' that the customs should be provided with lists of works likely to be printed abroad than with complete lists of all copyright publications. 'Directions in conformity with the acts of last session', Gladstone wrote, 'will be sent to all colonies.' However the relevant clause in the customs act, no doubt by an oversight in drafting, was limited to the United Kingdom: it did not apply as Gladstone seemed to suppose to the colonies. And the colonies—at least the recalcitrant children of the mother of parliaments in those north American provinces which now constitute the dominion of Canada —were spry enough to take advantage of an apparent inconsistency in the law. For years the Canadian provinces and the West Indian islands, avid of cheap reading matter, had relied on imports of books from the United States. The idea that good cheap British literary works of lasting benefit to the new world should be seized and destroyed by custom officers merely because they came from the United States was to them both irrational and oppressive. Evasion of customs with the connivance of officers was—I had almost said customary: it was certainly both widespread and undisguised. Moreover the local legislatures sought to legitimate it by enactments of their own, justifying the exclusion of expensive editions and the importation, not of piracies as such, but of books the poor colonials could afford. Another customs act was

† I owe the text of this letter and other details in this lecture to the John Murray of to-day. Murray's letters to Gladstone are in the British Museum.

accordingly passed in Westminster in 1845 both to extend the 1842 regulations to the colonies and to discipline the recalcitrant children. This act declared null and void 'all laws, bye-laws, usages or customs, in practice, or endeavoured or pretended to be in force or practice' in any of the British possessions in America which were 'in any-wise repugnant' to the statutes of Westminster.

Westminster was fighting a losing battle. Piratical reprints of sermons and poems, histories and dictionaries, as well as of the novels of Dickens and Bulwer-Lytton and Harrison Ainsworth, produced in the United States at prices with which British pub-lishers could not compete, continued to flood into the provinces and islands; and urgent representations alike from the governors and the customs officers flooded into Whitehall. In 1846 the colonial office and the board of trade admitted the force of the colonists' arguments 'as tending to shew the injurious effects upon our more distant colonists of the operation of the imperial law of copyright'. So in 1847 was passed what came to be known as the foreign reprints act. This gave the Queen authority to suspend the operation of the 1842 act and to express her royal approval of enactments of colonial legislatures admitting to colonies what would otherwise have been piratical reprints of British books. Her Majesty had to be satisfied that the interests of the copyright pro-prietors were adequately safeguarded. The safeguard was to be a duty on foreign-printed editions levied in colonial ports, a part of the duty being in theory reserved for the British author or publisher. In the outcome, as the royal commission was able to demonstrate in 1878, few authors or publishers received a penny from this source.

Before turning to the two remaining copyright acts in the first group, passed in 1844 and 1852—acts regulating relations with other sovereign states—I want to describe the project of one publisher to take advantage of the legislation designed to exclude piracies from the colonies. The publisher was John Murray and the project was 'Mr. Murray's Colonial and Home Library, dedicated, by per-mission, to the Right Honourable Lord Stanley, Secretary of State for the Colonies, and the Right Honourable W. E. Gladstone,

President of the Board of Trade'. In a letter to John Murray in February 1843 Gladstone had written that the recent proceedings of the legislature—that is the copyright and customs acts of 1842— would be fruitless unless the law were seconded by such modes of publication as would allow the public at home and in the colonies to obtain new and popular English books at moderate prices. If authors and publishers would agree to such modes of publication he foresaw 'a great extension of our book-trade as well as much advantage to literature'. (The president of the board of trade evidently put the economy before the encouragement of learning.) But it was up to the book trade to adapt themselves to the prevailing circumstances: otherwise, Gladstone wrote, 'we shall relapse into . . . the old state of things: the law will be first evaded, and then relaxed'. This is precisely what did happen: the foreign reprints act of 1847 was a relaxation after only four years of the very laws that Gladstone was hoping in 1843 to see enforced with the cooperation of Mr. Murray and his fellows in the trade.

In the following August Murray wrote to Gladstone seeking an interview in order to discuss two questions. Whether the interview took place is not on record: it does not very much matter as the questions were adumbrated in Murray's letter. The first point for discussion was one about which I have little information. Reading between the lines it appears that, since Westminster's measures to keep cheap United States piracies out of the colonies, some publishers in Britain were beginning to take over this illicit trade abetted by those colonial legislatures which were legislating against expensive books as 'impediments to intellectual advancement'. It appears also that certain London booksellers were planning to reimport these cheap British piracies from the colonies for sale in England. Murray sought Gladstone's help in preventing this. Secondly Murray had hatched a scheme, exclusively he believed his own, not yet publicly announced, and one which he was 'determined at all risques to commence'. He wished to lay his scheme for a 'colonial library' before the president of the board of trade and to ask permission to dedicate it to him.

Now Murray was one of the most reputable and conservative

of publishers—none of your piratical Bohns or Bogues or Teggs. He had no doubt deeply pondered Gladstone's advice that the book trade should second the efforts of the legislature to purge the colonies of pirates. As a business man he did not enjoy seeing the Bohns and Routledges and others eating into his profits on the slightest legal pretext by putting out cheap piracies of foreign authors' books for the copyright of which his father had paid good money. Nor did he like losing good money by American infringements in the colonies of his British authors' copyrights. Hence his new scheme. Murray also told the Governor of Upper Canada that the democratic tendency of native American publications was sapping the principles and loyalty of colonial subjects of the Queen.

A man should not be judged by his prospectuses. Nevertheless I shall quote at some length, partly *verbatim* and partly in paraphrase, from the prospectus (fig. 7) of the Colonial and Home Library: for in spite of its highfalutin language it gives an excellent picture of the situation in the colonies as seen by a London publisher, and of the dilemmas of the publisher, in the early 1840s.

The recent acts of parliament, the prospectus explained, would protect British authors and publishers by the rigid and entire exclusion of foreign pirated editions. They would for the first time if properly enforced direct into the right channel the colonies' demand for English literature—'a demand of which our authors and publishers have hitherto been deprived by the introduction of piracies from the United States, France and Belgium'. In order that 'the highly intelligent and educated population of our colonies' might not suffer from 'the withdrawal of their accustomed supplies of books' and from a consequent 'check to their intellectual advancement', Mr. Murray had determined to publish a series of attractive and useful works by approved authors, partly original works and partly new editions of popular publications, 'at a rate which shall place them within reach of the means, not only of the colonists, but also of a large portion of the less wealthy classes at home'. (The price was in fact 2s. per monthly half-volume, later increased to 2s. 6d., some works extending to two or more half-volumes.) The colonial library would 'furnish the settler in the

𝔇𝔢𝔡𝔦𝔠𝔞𝔱𝔢𝔡, 𝔟𝔶 𝔓𝔢𝔯𝔪𝔦𝔰𝔰𝔦𝔬𝔫,

TO

THE RIGHT HONOURABLE LORD STANLEY
SECRETARY OF STATE FOR THE COLONIES;

AND

THE RIGHT HONOURABLE W. E. GLADSTONE,
PRESIDENT OF THE BOARD OF TRADE.

MR. MURRAY'S
COLONIAL AND HOME LIBRARY.

The main object of this undertaking is to furnish the inhabitants of the Colonies of Great Britain with the highest literature of the day, consisting partly of Original Works, partly of New Editions of Popular Publications, at the lowest possible price. It is called for in consequence of the Acts which have recently passed the British Parliament for the protection of the rights of British authors and publishers, by the rigid and entire exclusion of foreign pirated editions. These Acts, if properly enforced, will, for the first time, direct into the right channel the demand of the Colonies for English Literature : a demand of which our authors and publishers have hitherto been deprived, by the introduction of piracies from the United States, France, and Belgium. In order, therefore, that the highly intelligent and educated population of our Colonies may not suffer from the withdrawal of their accustomed supplies of books, and with a view to obviate the complaint that a check might in consequence be raised to their intellectual advancement, Mr. Murray has determined to publish a series of attractive and useful works, by approved authors, at a rate which shall place them within reach of the means not only of the colonists, but also of a large portion of the less wealthy classes at home, who will thus benefit by the widening of the market for our literature : and the " Colonial Library " will consequently be so conducted that it may claim to be considered as a " Library for the Empire." Owing to the very low price placed upon the numbers of this series, the undertaking can succeed only if it meets with strenuous support from the Colonial Government at home and abroad, in giving effect to *the law*, and in supporting the just rights of British genius, industry, and manufactures, by preventing illicit importation of foreign reprints. It is also necessary for its progress and success, that it be favoured with the patronage of the reading public in all parts of the British dominions ; and the chief aim and object of the publisher will be to render it worthy of their countenance.

Mr. Murray's " Colonial Library " will furnish the settler in the backwoods of America, and the occupant of the remotest cantonment of our Indian dominions, with the resources of recreation and instruction at a moderate price, together with many new books, within a short period of their appearance in England ; while the student and lover of literature at home, who has hitherto been content with the loan of a book from a book-club, or has been compelled to wait for its tardy perusal from the shelves of a circulating library, or perhaps has satisfied his curiosity by the scanty extracts in magazines or reviews, may now become possessed of the work itself, at the moment of its publication, and at a cost little beyond that entailed by either of the methods above-mentioned. He may at the same time lay up a permanent Library in a condensed and portable form.

It will no doubt prove a source of satisfaction to the lovers of English literature in the Colonies to know that they are enjoying the intellectual gratification of the works of native authors, without doing any wrong or injury to those authors' interests.

Persons residing in the distant quarters of the world to which the dominions of Queen Victoria extend, and unacquainted with the practical system of authorship and publication, may probably never have dreamed that they were doing an act of injustice to the authors, for whose works they perhaps entertained the sincerest devotion, by the encouragement they have been in the habit of giving to foreign reprints. But the reason why the American, French, and other pirates of British copyrights have no difficulty in producing cheap books is, that *they pay nothing to the authors of them*. They cannot publish the works of their own authors at the same rate. But besides availing themselves of the genius and hard toil of others without making them any return, the cost of printing and paper in those countries is nearly one-half less than in England.

On the other hand, the pirated editions, owing to the hurried manner in which they are got up (being generally printed within twenty-four hours of the receipt of the English edition), and in order to save the (in England necessary) expense of common revision, are full of the grossest blunders, which must often interfere with the correct understanding of the work.

The series of Works designed to appear in Mr. Murray's " Colonial and Home Library" will be selected for their acknowledged merit, and will be exclusively such as are calculated to please the most extensive circles of readers. They will be printed most carefully, in a superior style, and on good paper.

SOUTHEY'S LIFE OF NELSON,
CONTAINING THE AUTHOR'S LAST ADDITIONS AND CORRECTIONS,
Price TWO SHILLINGS,
WILL FORM
No. I. OF MURRAY'S COLONIAL AND HOME LIBRARY,
And will be published on the 1st of October.

" The Life of Nelson is, beyond all doubt, the most perfect and the most delightful of Mr. Southey's works. No writer, perhaps, ever lived whose talents so precisely qualified him to write the history of the great naval hero."
MACAULAY, in *The Edinburgh Review.*

*** *Country Booksellers may be supplied with this Prospectus on applying through their London Correspondents.* (1062)

FIG. 7.

backwoods of America'—that is the northern provinces—'and the
occupant of the remotest cantonment of our Indian dominions
with the resources of recreation and instruction at a moderate price,
together with many new books, within a short period of their
appearance in England'. On one hand Mr. Murray sought the
support of the colonial government at home and abroad for 'the
just rights of British genius, industry and manufactures, by preventing illicit importation of foreign reprints'; on the other, he
had no doubt that it would 'prove a source of satisfaction to lovers
of English literature in the colonies to know that they are enjoying
the intellectual gratification of the works of native authors, without doing any wrong or injury to those authors' interests'. The
prospectus continues:

> Persons residing in the distant quarters of the world to which the domi-
> nions of Queen Victoria extend, and unacquainted with the practical system
> of authorship and publication, may probably never have dreamed that they
> were doing an act of injustice to the authors, for whose works they perhaps
> entertained the sincerest devotion, by the encouragement they have been in
> the habit of giving to foreign reprints. But the reason why the American,
> French, and other pirates of British copyrights have no difficulty in producing
> cheap books is, that *they pay nothing to the authors of them*. They cannot pub-
> lish the works of their own authors at the same rate. But besides availing
> themselves of the genius and hard toil of others without making them any
> return, the cost of printing and paper in those countries is nearly one-half
> less than in England.
> On the other hand, the pirated editions, owing to the hurried manner in
> which they are got up (being generally printed within twenty-four hours
> of the receipt of the English edition), and in order to save the (in England
> necessary) expense of common revision, are full of the grossest blunders,
> which must often interfere with the correct understanding of the work.

Mr. Murray's colonial library would be printed most carefully, in
a superior style, and on good paper.

If Mr. Murray assessed correctly the literary tastes of the backwoods and cantonments those tastes were somewhat restricted. Of
his final list of forty-nine titles in thirty-seven volumes more than
half were books of travel or travellers' tales and more than half of
the remainder were works of history. Fewer than a third were new

books. Even Herman Melville's fictional *Typee* and *Omoo* which first appeared in this series were advertised simply as 'Melville's *Marquesas Islands*' and 'Melville's *South Seas*'. Murray's declared intention had been to produce 'a series of works as entertaining as romances, but conveying at the same time sound information'. He had apparently inherited his father's distaste for straight fiction.

After six years the library was brought to an abrupt end. An earlier change of title from 'Colonial and Home' to 'Home and Colonial' is perhaps an indication of which market had proved the more remunerative. The library had been according to a vale-dictory announcement 'an unabated success'. Why then was it stopped after, of all odd numbers, thirty-seven volumes? One answer is offered in the valediction:

Mr. Murray, anxious to guard against the objection of overloading the subscribers with too large and cumbrous a series of books of one size, has decided on concluding the work with its thirty-seventh volume. He is thus able to offer to the public a compact and portable work, the bulk of which does not exceed the compass of a single shelf, or of one trunk, suited for all classes and all climates.

The publisher was evidently hoping to sell off complete sets of his unsold stock to prospective emigrants or others.

It is touching to think of Mr. Murray brooding over the bursting cabin-trunks of emigrant younger sons and pioneers of empire. However he told Mr. Gladstone another story. The 'real cause' of the failure of English publishers to supply colonial needs, he explained, was the large cost of the copyrights of the sort of books put out by the better publishing houses in competition with American piracies—piracies 'produced without paying copyright, corrections, freight, or duty, which it was impossible to contend against at any remunerative price. I made the experiment with my Colonial Library of giving new copyright works at the lowest price, but was forced to abandon it through the slight encourage-ment either at home or in the colonies.' So ended a gallant venture.

I must now return from the colonies to Europe and to the two effective statutes concerning international copyright in the first fifteen years of Victoria's reign.

The act of 1844 while it repealed Victoria's first abortive act had the same object in view, namely the object of empowering the Queen in council to enter into agreements with foreign states for the exchange of privileges of copyright. The first convention under this act was signed with Prussia in 1846 and provided that the other states of the Prussian *Zollverein*, and any states later joining the *Zollverein*, should have the right to accede to it—which in the course of the next decade they all did. Briefly the contracting governments agreed to grant the same protection and remedies to each other's subjects as to their own, provided that the books had been first published and copyright in the author's country and provided that copies were registered and delivered to libraries according to the law of the foreign country. Registration in this instance was compulsory, not permissive. The convention also prescribed lower rates of import duty than were imposed on books imported into either state from other countries.

The last act in the first group was the international copyright act of 1852. The primary purpose was to carry into effect a reciprocal convention with France agreed in the previous year. The convention itself differed in many respects from those with the German states and formed a model for later conventions, with Belgium in 1855, with Spain in 1857, and with the States of Sardinia in 1861. The Anglo-French convention brought into prominence for the first time the problem of translated works, and there can be read between the lines the French negotiators' wish to curb the British playwrights' habit of adapting French farces without leave, acknowledgment or payment for the English stage. The convention also makes for the first time the stipulation, repeated in the act, that a proprietor wishing to reserve his right of translation must signify his intention on his title-page or, if there is no title-page (as with a periodical contribution), 'on some conspicuous part of the work'.

The countries with which Britain had reciprocal copyright agreements between the 1850s and the Berne convention of 1887 can be numbered on the fingers of one hand: Germany, France, Belgium, Spain and part of Italy. On the whole the conventions brought greater advantage to Britain than to the other contracting states. Owing to a growing demand for British books on the continent more British authors were likely to reap the rewards of publication abroad, whether in English or in translation, than the number of continental writers who would take advantage of reciprocal privileges in Britain. But there was another side to the balance-sheet. There were no conventions with half of Europe or with Russia or with the United States. In all these countries, where the demand for British books was greater than the British demand for their books, editions generally termed piratical could legitimately be printed or imported; and some of these editions chiefly of United States but also of Dutch origin continued to circulate widely as piracies in the convention states and in the British territories oversea.

So much for statute law and some of its intentions, successes and failures up to 1852. What next of the status of the foreign author? —a character known to the law as an 'alien ami', spelled indifferently *ami* or *amy* and pronounced in lawyer's argot like a female personal name. On this subject Queen Anne had inevitably been silent. But as early as 1777 in the case of *Bach* v. *Longman* it was held that a foreigner who came to England and first published a work here could sue for infringement of copyright. Johann Christian Bach was a composer. Most of the leading cases on international copyright in the mid-nineteenth century were concerned with musical publications.

That a foreigner who was resident in or came to Britain could claim copyright seems to have been taken for granted for more than half a century after Bach's case. Washington Irving undoubtedly acted on this assumption. Irving spent long periods in Europe between 1804 and 1832. Many years later, in 1850, when John Murray sued Henry Bohn for infringements of the copyrights which Irving had verbally assigned to his father, a series of affidavits was sworn on both sides of the Atlantic the purpose of which was to prove that the assignments were valid and the copyrights protected. One point at issue was whether various of the books, including Irving's *Sketch Book* which had appeared in instalments in America over several months on either side of British book publication, were in fact first published in Britain. This had seemed relevant in the 1820s and 30s. Irving was able to reply that he wrote the *Sketch Book* in England; *Bracebridge Hall* and one other book partly in England and partly in France; two other books in England and Spain; and several partly in England and partly in the United States. Incidentally in 1850 Bohn— astutely, you may think, if your sympathies are not engaged— raised the question whether Irving could in law be regarded as an *ami*: he had served as an *aide-de-camp* to the governor of New York State shortly after the British had burnt down the capitol at Washington in 1814. This meant, Bohn alleged in his particulars concerning alienage, that Irving had borne arms against King George.

In 1835, to quote only one example of a law-suit immediately before Victoria came to the throne, it was decided in the case of *D'Almaine* v. *Boosey*, both music publishers, that a foreigner could assign his copyright to a British publisher even though he did not visit our shores: the publisher could claim protection and it made no difference, said Lord Abinger delivering judgment, whether the proprietor of the work had composed it himself or had bought it from a foreigner. Similarly in the year after the first abortive copy-right act of Victoria, in the case of *Bentley* v. *Foster* over a novel by Fenimore Cooper, Vice-Chancellor Shadwell said that in his opinion protection was given to a work first published in this country whether it was written abroad by a foreigner or not: if an alien friend wrote a book whether here or abroad and 'gave the British public the advantage of his industry and knowledge' by publishing it here first, the work became a 'domiciled publication' entitled to the protection of British copyright law. If this was so it was open to any American novelist to obtain British copyright by ensuring that his novel was published in Britain one day before it appeared in America: he need not cross the Atlantic to achieve this. This was the year in which Captain Marryat learnt that even twelve months' residence in the United States would not earn copyright protection for an English novelist unless he were prepared to change his nationality.

The view that a publication could become domiciled here though the foreign author was neither domiciled nor resident, nor even a visitor, was upheld in several decisions in the courts of common pleas and Queen's bench in the 1840s though with certain reservations. The need for first publication here was never in doubt, and in 1848 in *Cocks* v. *Purday* the further point was for the first time decided, only to be hotly contested some years later, that 'contemporaneous' publication abroad did not defeat a foreigner's right. In the following year however, whereas in January Boosey obtained an injunction in the Queen's bench restraining Davidson, a rival publisher, from publishing five arias from Bellini's opera *La Somnambula*, in June he lost a case in the exchequer against Purday, another rival, over ten arias from the same opera. In the latter case much play was made with 'contemporaneity' of publication. Of the ten arias in dispute nine had been published in 1831 in Milan at nine o'clock of a June morning—the equivalent of 8.20 Greenwich mean time—but they had not appeared in London until between noon and one o'clock on the same day: with the tenth Boosey could prove two months' priority over Milan. The question whether the law took account of fractions of a day, however, did not need to be decided. Boosey lost his case on a more general ground. The head-notes in the official reports of the two *La Somnambula* cases read as follows:

Boosey v. *Davidson* [Queen's bench, January].
The assignee of a foreign author of a work published in England, without having been published abroad, has copyright in this country.
Boosey v. *Purday* [Court of exchequer, June].
A foreign author, residing and composing his work abroad, sending it to this country and first publishing it here, does not acquire any copyright in England.

The latter judgment proceeded on the assumption that the legislature must be considered *prima facie* to have legislated for its own subjects, and that its object clearly was not to encourage the importation of foreign works and their first publication in Britain but to promote the cultivation of the intellect of its subjects. This was tantamount to saying that no alien *ami* at all could claim protection in Britain.

These virtually contradictory decisions, both resting on common law, delivered within six months of one another had the effect of turning yesterday's piracies into today's legitimate though unauthorized publications. It was against this confused background that Mr. Murray's legal advisers were preparing suits against Mr. Bohn over the Washington Irving copyrights and against Mr. Routledge for alleged piracy of two more recent books, Melville's *Typee* and *Omoo*. The judgment in Boosey against Purday was in June 1849. Notices of injunctions were served on Bohn and Routledge in July 1850. Letters and affidavits were sailing across the Atlantic with Irving first appointing Mr. Murray his attorney in any copyright legislation in England and later withdrawing for fear of compromising his character as 'a native born and thoroughly loyal American citizen'. The suits in equity came on before Vice-Chancellor Knight Bruce on 7 and 8 August and were dismissed with leave to the plaintiff, if he thought fit, to pursue his claim at common law.

That the plaintiff did think fit in the following spring, after incurring considerable extra expense, was probably due to the judgment in *Ollendorf* v. *Black*, also in chancery, in December. *Boosey* v. *Purday* had turned on the alleged copyright of an alien residing abroad. Professor Ollendorf on the other hand, a Frenchman, was on a visit to England when his French grammar was first published by Whittaker at 12s., only to be pirated by Black in a 5s. 6d. edition imported from Frankfurt-am-Main. The fact of British residence sufficiently distinguished the case and enabled Knight Bruce to dissent with eloquence from the obscurantist view of the exchequer barons.

Can any conclusion be imagined more injurious to literature in general [the vice-chancellor asked in the course of his judgment] than the decision in *Boosey versus Purday*? Surely literature is of no country, and the object of the act of parliament must be to promote learning generally. That decision is an unfortunate one for literature in this country; for is it not a benefit that the learned men of other countries should publish their works here?

Emboldened by this stirring rhetoric Mr. Murray began proceedings in the Queen's bench in May 1851, only to drop them after Bohn's counsel had applied for leave to amend his plea on the first day of the trial. Precisely why he dropped them is not clear though it is certain that he had other troubles on his hands—the great 'Bookselling Question' for example—and that he had lost money in recent years on Washington Irving and had kept few of his books in print. He had also spent a good deal on preparing litigation in a cause in which his legal advisers cannot have had much confidence. Anyhow he withdrew his suits against Bohn and Routledge and sold his Irving copyrights and printed stocks to Bohn for two thousand guineas, reserving only his right to continue to publish certain titles in his colonial library.

Murray's capitulation was unfortunate for two reasons. In the first place it was unfortunate for Murray himself. His actions were being heard by Lord Campbell who in his next judgment came down emphatically in favour of the alien *ami*. In the second place it was unfortunate for posterity: full argument in court of a case involving Washington Irving and Herman Melville would have been pregnant with interest and instruction for the twentieth-century bibliographer and historian of publishing. It is curiously ironical that through Murray's withdrawal the rights or lack of rights in Britain of American poets, novelists, essayists, philosophers, historians and other writers up to 1891 should have rested largely on decisions in the courts in the forties and fifties about the overture to *Fra Diavolo*, composed by 'one Auber, a Frenchman, at Paris' in 1829; a cavatina from *La Somnambula*, composed by 'one Bellini, an Italian, at Milan' (an Austrian city) in 1831; a waltz composed by Joseph Labitzky of Carlsbad and sold to Joseph Hoffmann of Prague in 1842; and a teach-yourself-French-in-six-months text-book by Henri Godefroy Ollendorf of Paris, published in 1843.

Henry Bohn, preparing his defence against Murray, had intended to rely among other precedents on the decision of Baron Rolfe in another music copyright case, Boosey against Jefferys, which had gone against Boosey as assign of an alien. But in that summer of 1851, just after Murray had decided to give up the fight, Boosey won his appeal on a writ of error in the court of exchequer chamber, Lord Campbell presiding. Having premised that an alien *ami* domiciled in Britain though neither naturalized nor a denizen might acquire a copyright here, and that even if only on a temporary visit if he had composed and published a poem here he might acquire copyright in it, Campbell went on to question whether it could make any difference if he composed his poem abroad and brought it with him, or even if having memorized it abroad he first wrote it out in England. 'Where', his Lordship asked, 'can be the necessity for his crossing from Calais to Dover before giving directions for the publication of his work and entering it at Stationers' Hall?' The court ruled that wherever a foreign author was residing first publication in the United Kingdom made him 'an author within the meaning of our statutes for the encouragement of learning'. So now we are back to Square One.

Campbell's judgment was a triumph for the liberal forces, as they considered themselves—those who believed that all authors of all nations should have equal rights before British law. It was correspondingly a defeat for those other liberal forces—and they included philanthropical societies and retail booksellers as well as piratical publishers—who were campaigning for cheap books for the masses. Routledge and Bohn who had forced Murray to capitulate only a month or two before were now themselves driven to compromise similar actions which were pending, actions brought against them by Richard Bentley over copyrights of Washington Irving and Fenimore Cooper. Their supposedly legitimate thefts had turned to piracies overnight. For popular British authors also this was indirectly a defeat. By giving unrestricted privilege to alien, especially American, authors whose publishers sent plates or advance sheets to Britain for first publication this decision removed half the incentive from American authors and publishers to press for a reciprocal convention between the United States and the United Kingdom, a convention that would have brought rewards to British novelists and have removed the 'monstrous injustice' at the mere thought of which, Dickens said, his blood rose to boiling point.

One must be sorry for Routledge and Bohn, not knowing from one month to the next on which common they might safely graze their cattle. Pity the poor publisher, I said last week. And pity the writer of legal text-books too, for that matter: Peter Burke for example. His admirable little book† inspired by the Anglo-French convention and the enabling act of 1852 went to press late that year with the assertion that the judgment on appeal in *Boosey* v. *Jefferys* had 'brought the subject to a clear understanding' and had 'finally decided' the status of the alien *ami*. Mr. Burke could not know— nor could Murray or Bentley, Routledge or Bohn, let alone Jefferys and Boosey and a score of other publishers of books and music, and scores of American publishers and authors with the gate- way to British copyright now thrown open to them—none of these could know that within two years Lord Campbell's momentous judgment, 'finally decided', would be reversed in the House of Lords.

Once again the decision, and this a decision of the highest tri- bunal in the land, rested on the assumption that Queen Anne must have legislated for her own subjects. But 'subjects' was at least now interpreted as including all persons who being within Queen Victoria's dominions owed her an allegiance, no matter how tem- porary. Copyright commenced at the instant of publication. Provided the author was within the Queen's dominions at that instant, even if he had only come for the express purpose of securing his right, his right was secure. Hence the large number of United States citizens who came to Britain, or crossed the frontier into Canada, or nipped over to the West Indies, between 1854 and 1891 on their publication days—Hawthorne and Oliver Wendell Holmes, Mrs. Stowe and Louisa Alcott and Frances Hodgson Burnett among them.

We have now by a mixture of statute and case law arrived at a position, in 1854 and for nearly forty years to come, where foreign authors can be divided into two groups. A national of any of the

† *The Law of Copyright between England and France . . . in English and French*, 1852.

convention countries—let us say France—if he has secured copy-right according to the laws of his own country, can claim it or assign it to a publisher in Britain even if his book is not first pub-lished in Britain. A national of a non-convention country—say Italy before 1861, or the United States—can only, and a little un-certainly, obtain British copyright by residence and first publica-tion in a British territory. Yet it is not quite as simple as that. Reciprocal privilege did not mean equal privilege. Each state re-tained its own domestic laws and those laws differed from state to state. In Britain from 1842 onwards copyright in a book published in an author's lifetime lasted for forty-two years or until seven years after his death, whichever should be the longer; in France it passed to his widow for her life and to his children for a further twenty years. A British author's assigns were protected in France for the French period whereas a Frenchman's were protected in England only for the British.

Moreover in France on the principle of *à tous la liberté* a national of any state could obtain French copyright merely by publication and deposit, and the question arose whether having done so, and supposing him to be an Italian or an American, he could under the umbrella of the Anglo-French convention claim British copyright (as a Frenchman could) without residence and first publication in Britain. This possible loophole in international law presented itself in 1855 to the ingenious mind of the Italian Giovanni Domenico ('John') Ruffini. Ruffini lived in Paris and wrote in English. His anonymous novel *Lorenzo Benoni* had been published by Con-stable's in Edinburgh in 1853 with considerable success, and it had been reprinted without authority in a cheap series in London, a matter of some concern to both Ruffini and Constable. Constable thereupon arranged for the Italian's next novel, *Doctor Antonio*, to be first registered in Paris and published by Galignani in order to ensure for it when reprinted in Edinburgh the British protection which Ruffini could not as a non-convention national directly obtain. I suspect, though I cannot be certain, that the reverse pro-cess gave continental protection to the American Nathaniel Haw-thorne when he was resident in England.

III

CONTINENTAL: MAINLY TAUCHNITZ

THE trade in books between Britain and the continent is a large subject and I propose to concentrate only upon one aspect of it. Translations will not be mentioned, and little concerning France will be added to what appeared in the last lecture. The first half of the nineteenth century up to the Anglo-French convention of 1852 was treated in a scholarly article contributed to the *Library* in December 1961 by Mr. Giles Barber. Mr. Barber's subject was ostensibly the Paris firm of Galignani but he ranged over the wider field of British and American books printed for other French and Belgian publishers and sold not only on the continent but piratically in Britain and America.

International copyright first became a live issue in Europe in the middle 1830s. There was hardly a capital in Europe where the subject was not canvassed. It is commonly held that the first international copyright act passed anywhere was that of Queen Victoria dated 31 July 1838. In fact on 11 June 1837, some days before Victoria became Queen, the King of Prussia signed a law† extending copyright protection to foreign works if the foreign state reciprocated. Six years before Britain's first international convention (with Prussia in 1846) Austria had established reciprocal copyright with Sardinia, and Holland with France. Under the act of 1844 Britain signed conventions with several German states in the forties, and under the act of 1852 with France, Belgium, Spain and other German states in the fifties, and with the States of Sardinia in 1861. The agreement with Sardinia—covering, that is, the areas then ruled by Victor Emmanuel—was never formally extended to the rest of Italy. A domestic copyright law‡ was enacted in Victor Emmanuel's

† No. 1840. *Gesetz zum Schutze des Eigentums an Werken der Wissenschaft und Kunst gegen Nachdruck und Nachbildung*, § 38. On 29 November 1837 Prussia adopted by *Publikations-Patent* (No. 1839) a resolution of the *Deutsche Bundesversammlung* embodying uniform copyright principles within the *Bund*.

‡ No. 2337, *Legge sui diritti spettanti agli autori delle opere dell'ingegno*.

enlarged dominion in 1865 and others followed in Venice and Mantua in 1867 and finally in Rome in 1870: but reciprocal copyright with Britain after the unification of Italy, if it was effective at all, seems to have been a matter of international courtesy rather than of international law. It was these countries—Germany, France, Belgium, Spain and Italy—with Switzerland, Tunis and Haiti added, that adopted the Berne convention in 1887. That was a year of fiftieth anniversaries: Queen Victoria's jubilee, the fiftieth anniversary of the tabling in parliament of Britain's first international copyright act, and the fiftieth birthday of the publishing house of Bernhard Tauchnitz of Leipzig.

Christian Bernhard Tauchnitz, later the Freiherr von Tauchnitz, came of landed Saxon stock. His father being dead he was apprenticed to his uncle Karl Tauchnitz, printer and publisher of bibles and ancient classics, reputed to have set up the first stereotyping plant in Germany. Karl died in 1836. Bernhard, the nephew and future baron, established his own printing and publishing firm in 1837 when he was under twenty-one. He immediately laid plans for entering the continental market for cheap reprints of British and American copyright books. There were plenty of other firms in this market, notably on his own home ground Fleischer of Leipzig who before Tauchnitz was ready had published the 'complete works', of which there were then only four, 'of Charles Dickens, in English'. Tauchnitz almost certainly from the start had his eye on the growing movement in Europe and the United States towards the establishment of international copyright and on the advantage of being early in the field. But when the Tauchnitz 'Collection of British Authors' made its début in September 1841 there were as yet no international conventions, and I am reluctantly forced to the assumption that in its first two years the publications in the Tauchnitz collection were unauthorized.

I say 'reluctantly forced' partly in view of the character that I hope to build up of the baron as the honest broker, but also because in a centenary publication in 1937 the firm of Tauchnitz claimed that 'from the first' the founder 'required the written authority of his authors, and he paid for it'. This claim is, I suspect, the result of summarizing or conflating sentences in an earlier *Festschrift*. However that may be, in 1841 and 1842 Tauchnitz besides the works of Goldsmith, Byron and Tom Moore published in his collection twelve novels by Bulwer-Lytton, three by Captain Marryat, two titles each by Dickens and Fenimore Cooper and one by G. P. R. James. Other books by these writers followed in the early months of 1843. There is no evidence that Tauchnitz had any contact as early as this with any of his British or American authors or with their British or American publishers. The earliest letters he preserved from Dickens and Marryat, and they read like first letters, are dated 1843. On 19 July of that year the following paragraph appeared under a London date-line in the *Leipziger Zeitung*:

In the last few days a German publisher, Herr Bernhard Tauchnitz of Leipzig, has concluded agreements for continental editions of English works in the original language, authorized by the authors—a first step towards recognition of English literary copyright on the German book-market. It is understood that three new books, by Bulwer, James and Lady Blessington, have already been given to Herr Tauchnitz to publish.

An editorial note added, 'The editor has just seen the announcement of these works in the *Börsenblatt*. There is therefore no doubt that this agreeable news is true.'

It was true indeed. Tauchnitz had visited London, had had conversations with Messrs. Longmans and other publishers and had addressed a letter to a number of British authors in the following terms:

The wish to publish the editions of new English works which I am bringing out in Germany, with the authority and sanction of the authors, is the reason of my now addressing you.

Allow me, however, to remark that I as well as any other publisher in Germany have at present the right to embark in such undertakings without any permission from the Authors; and that my propositions arise solely from the wish thereby to make the first step towards a literary relationship between England and Germany, and towards an extension of the rights of Copyright, and to publish my editions in accordance with these rights.

I therefore beg to offer you—[here he filled in the sum he was offering for a book or books]. For this you will give me your authority for publishing my edition for the Continent. I do not in any way claim the right of sending my edition to England or to your Colonies, and I will not in any way attempt to hinder the sale of the English original editions in Germany. I cannot doubt that you will immediately accept my offer, and I hope that this first attempt to establish a connection with the Classical Authors of England will lead to a long and advantageous relationship on both sides.

The form of contract which Tauchnitz offered at this time read:

It is agreed between Lady Blessington and Mr. Bernhard Tauchnitz of Leipzig that Lady Blessington will give to Mr. Tauchnitz her express sanction to publish an edition in English of her future works, and that Lady Blessington will give no similar sanction to any other German publisher.

Among the authors who accepted such offers in the next few months were not only Bulwer, G. P. R. James and Lady Blessington, but Dickens, Disraeli and Harrison Ainsworth. Between that summer of 1843 and the autumn of 1846 by which time Britain's conventions with Prussia and Saxony had been ratified Tauchnitz published upwards of forty volumes with the authority of British authors or their publishers.

Between 1846 and 1852 he could only acquire the exclusive right to sell British books in such German states as adhered to the Anglo-German convention. The remaining German states mattered little because the local market was too small to encourage the printing of unauthorized editions which were forbidden entry into the signatory states. With the Anglo-French convention in 1852 Tauchnitz was in a strong position to extend his range. He already had a market in France where his editions, authorized though not hitherto protected, were sold in competition with unauthorized editions of continental or American origin. It suited his British authors to allow him the sole right to sell their books in France as well as in Germany, and as more and more countries entered into reciprocal agreements his rights extended throughout the continent. There was some doubt at first, voiced to Tauchnitz by Macaulay, whether the Anglo-French convention had retrospective force in France—whether, that is, books copyright in Britain and Germany before 1852 could claim protection there. The point was settled by a decree of Louis Napoleon a short while later which forbade the distribution in France of all unauthorized editions of copyright works.

Most Tauchnitz volumes early and late bear on their title-pages or elsewhere in the volume some such words as 'author's edition', 'authorized edition', 'edition sanctioned by the author for continental circulation' or 'copyright edition'. It might be supposed that these phrases carried different and precise meanings: that authorization by a British author or his assign began in 1843, and that there could be no continental 'copyright edition' of a British book before 1846 and then only in Germany, or of an American book (unless first copyright in Britain or France) before 1891. The long run of early Tauchnitz volumes in the British Museum, a run not acquired however until 1868, lends support to this theory. For example in 1842 before his London visit Tauchnitz printed no assertion of Marryat's authorization of *Percival Keene*; in the next year after the visit Marryat's *Monsieur Violet* is described as 'sanctioned by the author'; and in 1846 his *Privateersman* is 'copyright'. Most American books are 'authorized' or as with one of Irving's 'published for the continent of Europe by contract with the author'.† Hawthorne's *Transformation*, 1860, is 'copyright' presumably because having secured British privilege by residence Hawthorne could claim continental privilege. Yet the pattern does not always work out like that. How is it that the British Museum copies of *Pickwick*, 1842, and *A Christmas Carol*, 1843, are designated 'copyright editions' at a time when no British author could claim copyright abroad?

This brings us up against what can only be called a shockingly bad habit bibliographically speaking of the good *Freiherr*, a habit that neither he nor his son ever outgrew. He would date his first printing correctly—though even to this there are exceptions—and

---

† Henry James was first introduced to the British public in a textually vicious yellow-back piracy of *The American* in December 1877. Soon afterwards Tauchnitz published an 'authorized edition' prefaced with the words, 'The present edition of *The American* is published with my full assent and in accordance with a liberal arrangement.—H. JAMES, Jr., Paris, Dec. 1877.'

he would then repeat the original date in impressions and even in revised editions printed many years later. The wrappers of Tauchnitz volumes often advertise books published years after the title-page dates: sometimes the wrappers themselves bear a much later date. An extreme example of which Dr. Jacob Blanck has told me is a copy of Hawthorne's *Transformation*, two volumes, with titles dated 1860 and wrappers 1906 and 1907. It is easy to assume that the sheets were printed at the earlier date and wrappered and issued later: but this can often be disproved at least as far as the prelims are concerned by a list on the half-title verso of books by the same author which the author had not even thought of writing at the date given on the facing page.

Nor is it safe to assume that the text sheets were printed from plates made from type set at the ostensible date. Of *Oliver Twist* Tauchnitz printed an edition in 1843 including the introduction which Dickens had published in London two years earlier. Professor Kathleen Tillotson when editing *Oliver Twist* for the Clarendon Dickens failed to find a complete copy. The copies she did trace are indeed dated 1843 but they contain the text that Dickens revised, and the new preface that he wrote, for publication in London in 1867. With one such copy, which to judge by its list of Dickens's works cannot have been printed before 1880, were bound up the preliminary leaves of an older edition printed in a different type and including the original introduction. But the title-page even of this relic carries the legend 'copyright edition', which in fact ought to mean that it belongs to an impression printed after 1846 of a first Tauchnitz edition of 1843.† One day on this theory a copy 'sanctioned by the author' should turn up. Such things do turn up if one looks in the right place. Only after seeing the British Museum's *Pickwick*, dated 1842 but with the

---

† These title-page legends are useful aids to identification. But if a book is properly described as 'authorized' or as 'copyright' in all its impressions the bibliographer will be hard put to identify the first printing. So will a collector who wants the positively first appearance of the revised text of Wilkie Collins's *The Woman in White* or of Henry James's *A Passionate Pilgrim*, or of a long letter of Dickens praising John Forster's *Life of Goldsmith* which Forster was too modest to include in his English editions but felt he could print with 'less impropriety' in Germany.

THE

POSTHUMOUS PAPERS

OF THE

PICKWICK CLUB,

CONTAINING A FAITHFUL RECORD OF THE

PERAMBULATIONS, PERILS, TRAVELS, ADVENTURES,

AND

SPORTING TRANSACTIONS OF THE CORRESPONDING
MEMBERS.

BY

BOZ (CHARLES DICKENS).

VOL. I.

WITH THE PORTRAIT OF THE AUTHOR.

LEIPZIG

BERNH. TAUCHNITZ JUN.

1842.

Fig. 8a. First title-page

THE

POSTHUMOUS PAPERS

OF THE

PICKWICK CLUB,

CONTAINING A FAITHFUL RECORD OF THE

PERAMBULATIONS, PERILS, TRAVELS, ADVENTURES,

AND

SPORTING TRANSACTIONS OF THE CORRESPONDING
MEMBERS.

BY

CHARLES DICKENS.

COPYRIGHT EDITION.

IN TWO VOLUMES.

VOL. I.

WITH THE PORTRAIT OF THE AUTHOR.

LEIPZIG

BERNHARD TAUCHNITZ

1842.

Fig. 8b. Second title-page

legend 'copyright edition', did I bethink myself of Bodley. Bodley's copy has no such legend (fig. 8), is printed from types which Tauchnitz later discarded and must almost certainly have been unauthorized. This view is not inconsistent with Tauchnitz's claim in a letter to John Forster that 'all Mr. Dickens's works have been published under agreement by me'. Tauchnitz went on to say that ·his intercourse with Dickens lasted from October 1843 to March 1870. In other words the agreements for *Pickwick* and other early books must have been for editions later than Tauchnitz's earliest printings.

Among exceptions to the rule that Tauchnitz's original title-page dates are correct Mr. Percy Muir pointed out in the *Book Collector* in 1955 that the three volumes of the Tauchnitz *David Copperfield* were dated 1849 though the second and third could not have appeared—Dickens had not finished writing them—before the spring and autumn respectively of 1850. Tauchnitz evidently set some of his editions of Dickens volume by volume from the monthly parts published by Bradbury & Evans. He did the same with Thackeray's *Pendennis* and he printed Trollope's *Lady Anna* from instalments of the *Fortnightly*, in each case misdating by normal bibliographical standards the last volume. Both Dickens and Thackeray in certain instances arranged not for the completed serial instalments but for proofs to be sent to Leipzig.† As early as 1844 Dickens was having early sheets of his books sent to German booksellers in order to 'facilitate German translations' and it is a fair assumption that he had them sent to Tauchnitz, one of whose gratuitous services to English writers was to arrange registration of their books in Berlin whether he intended to publish them himself or not. With *David Copperfield* Dickens promised proofs of the sixth number to Tauchnitz in October 1849 with a view to the publication of Tauchnitz's first volume in that month:

† In October 1848 Thackeray instructed Bradbury & Evans to send proofs of *The Great Hoggarty Diamond* to Williams & Norgate, Tauchnitz's London agents, for transmission to Tauchnitz. The first number of *Pendennis* was published in the following month, and in April 1849 Thackeray wrote promising Tauchnitz the two latest numbers. Within three months before his death in 1870 Dickens promised to send the numbers of *Edwin Drood* regularly.

he asked Bradbury & Evans to mark his corrections carefully on the proofs. It is always possible that the text of such marked proofs as reprinted by Tauchnitz differs from the text as published by Bradbury & Evans, supposing that Dickens made later corrections before his monthly numbers went finally to press in London. Editors of Dickens cannot escape the possibility—the fear, indeed the hope—that Tauchnitz volumes may contain variant readings.

In its jubilee year of 1887 the firm of Tauchnitz published a *Festschrift*. Prepared by the first baron's son Christian Karl Bernhard von Tauchnitz it is a solid octavo volume of 344 pages, by far the greater part being given up to the collection of British and American authors. Among other information it contains extracts of letters from some thirty authors dead by 1887. A briefer *Festschrift* celebrating the firm's seventy-fifth birthday adds extracts from authors who had died before 1912, and one briefer still carries the tally down to the centenary year of 1937.† The correspondents range from Dickens and Thackeray and George Eliot, Carlyle and Froude and Macaulay, through Tennyson, Meredith and Ouida, to writers of 1937 who sent centenary tributes—Wells, Walpole and Somerset Maugham; Stanley Baldwin, Lord Halifax (writing as chancellor of our university) and John Masefield. Unfortunately all the many hundreds of letters preserved by the firm together with their stock of publications, stereotype plates and printing plant were destroyed in an air raid on Leipzig in 1943.

The published extracts as might be expected are almost without exception flattering to the firm of Tauchnitz, to the two barons and to their successors—inevitably, for these were *Festschriften*. A cynic might suspect that the Tauchnitz archives contained, as most publishers' archives contain, letters of another colour. And no doubt they did. But there are other sources of information which confirm the trust and respect, often the affection, with which the

---

† The four publications are *Fünfzig Jahre der Verlagshandlung Bernhard Tauchnitz, 1837 bis 1887*, Leipzig, 1887; *Der Verlag Bernhard Tauchnitz, 1837–1912*, Leipzig, 1912; *The Harvest, being the record of 100 years of publishing, 1837–1937*, by *Bernhard Tauchnitz*, Leipzig, 1937; *Festschrift zum 125 jährigen Bestehen der Firma Bernhard Tauchnitz Verlag, 1837–1962*, Stuttgart, 1962.

founder was regarded by his English authors. There are letters of authors and publishers not addressed to Tauchnitz but referring to him, some published, some unpublished, and a few of Tauchnitz's own letters have survived. It is mainly to these sources though also to reports in newspapers that one must look for evidence of the terms on which the books in the collection were published: naturally enough the fees offered or paid for books were omitted from the extracts in the *Festschriften*.

The best known example of a personal relationship concerns Dickens who entrusted his sixteen-year-old son Charley to the Tauchnitz family for some months in 1853 to learn German. Charley, Dickens told Tauchnitz, should be 'treated like a gentleman, *though pampered in nothing*'. Assuring Angela Burdett-Coutts that Charley would be in good hands, Dickens wrote that the Chevalier Tauchnitz

is a publisher by profession (the largest, I believe, in Germany), but is a gentleman of great honour and integrity too. . . . I have had many transactions with him, referring to all my books, and am well acquainted with him personally, and with his thoroughly good reputation besides.

Harrison Ainsworth having revived the ancient custom of the Dunmow Flitch dedicated his novel *The Flitch of Bacon* to Herr and Frau Tauchnitz as 'the happiest couple I know'. Wilkie Collins dedicated *Miss or Mrs.?* to Tauchnitz 'in cordial remembrance of my relations with him as publisher and friend'. George Lewes late in life, in spite of what is yet to be revealed, wrote that both he and Mrs. Lewes—that is George Eliot—preserved such agreeable recollections of Tauchnitz that it would at all times be a pleasure to hear from him 'either on the subject of our books, or anything else'. And there were many others. More pertinent perhaps are Tauchnitz's financial relations with his authors and the type of agreement which he liked to make with them.

In the nineteenth century there were five principal types of contract between author and publisher.

First a book might be published on commission. The author retained his copyright. He paid the cost of printing, binding and advertising; stood the loss if the book did not pay for itself; reaped the profit if it did; and paid the publisher a commission—usually a percentage of the production costs. Secondly there was the system of half (or three-quarters) profits under which the costs were initially defrayed by the publisher but charged against the book; if sales failed to cover expenses the author was liable for half the expenses, plus in some contracts interest on the publisher's initial outlay; after the expenses had been met by sales author and publisher shared the profits equally. Thirdly there was the outright sale of the copyright to the publisher. He paid the author an agreed sum and that was that. He might lose on the deal or he might make a profit, perhaps so large a profit over the years that the author felt aggrieved. This system led to the successful author's idea that every publisher was a Barabbas: he forgot the publisher's risk and his losses on unsuccessful books. Fourthly there is what may be called a short lease; the publisher bought the right either to publish the book for a period of years or to publish an agreed number of copies or editions, after which the copyright reverted to the author.

Fifthly there was the royalty system under which the publisher took the risk and the author received a fixed sum, usually but not always a percentage of the advertised price of the book, for every copy sold. The percentage might vary according to the number of copies sold: by the time the system was thoroughly established fairly late in the nineteenth century contracts would specify different percentages for different editions of the same book—say 25 per cent for a three-decker, 10 per cent for an American one-volume edition, 15 per cent for a London cheap edition, and 3d. or 4d. a copy for a colonial edition. We take the royalty system so much for granted nowadays, and regard it as for most types of book the fairest division of spoils, that we tend to forget how slowly it evolved in the nineteenth century. It evolved even more slowly on the continent than in Britain and it was, or so Baron Tauchnitz believed, entirely uneconomic for the sort of cheap series that he specialized in.

So far as I know, Tauchnitz never published an English book on commission or on half-profits. It is true that some authors not included in his collection wrote to propose themselves for inclusion, but it seems unlikely that he would have asked them to bear the initial cost even if they had been willing. Charles Reade once suggested either 'a fixed sum or a share of the profits' but Tauchnitz chose to buy *It is Never too Late to Mend* outright. (Reade was very anxious to be included in what he called Tauchnitz's 'noble collection'. 'It contains', he wrote, 'many authors who are superior to me in merit and reputation, but it also contains the *entire works* of many writers who do not come up to my knee.') What the Tauchnitz father and son preferred can be deduced from their correspondence with individual authors. For it was with authors, as the father wrote in a letter to *The Times* in 1871, that he made most of his agreements unless they had previously sold their continental rights to their British publishers. Illustrations may be taken from a variety of authors, not in strict chronological order, beginning with Anthony Trollope. I forget which member of the staff drew my attention to the Trollope papers in Bodley, so I thank collectively all those members who have guided my footsteps with untiring patience and unfailing courtesy.

The first thing to note is that before the days of international copyright, although an author might enter into a contract with a foreign publisher, he could not sell the foreign rights in his book for he had none; and for many years after the first international conventions an author might well remain unaware that he now had foreign rights to sell. (The invincible ignorance of authors can be shewn to have been an embarrassment to some publishers and a source of profit to others.) British publishers continued to buy books outright or for a term of years without mention of oversea sales. Trollope's agreements with Newby in 1845, with Colburn in 1848–50, Longmans in 1854–7, and Bentley in 1857 are agreements for outright sale with no foreign strings attached. With *Doctor Thorne* in 1858 Trollope assigned to Edward Chapman of Chapman & Hall 'the copyright and all rights attaching thereto at home and abroad'. In the following year the formula for three other books was the same, but with a time limit of three years after which the copyright was to become the joint property of Trollope and Chapman & Hall. In all these instances it was open to the publishers to sell the continental rights to Tauchnitz, and they did. In 1860 a similar contract for *Orley Farm* contains this clause: 'Any amount resulting from the disposal of sheets of the work to foreign publishers to be the joint property of Mr. Trollope and Messrs. E. & F. Chapman'—that is Edward and Frederick Chapman 'trading under the firm of Chapman & Hall'. In 1863 the contract for *Can You Forgive Her?* stipulates that receipts from the disposal of sheets abroad should go to the author. With *Miss Mackenzie* in 1864 Trollope reserves to himself the copyright in all foreign countries.

A slightly different pattern appears in Trollope's agreement with Smith, Elder. In 1859 he sells them *Framley Parsonage* outright with no mention of foreign sales; in 1861 Smith, Elder buy *The Small House at Allington*, expressly reserving to themselves all profits from the sale of sheets to America and from the assignment of continental rights. In 1863 Trollope sells them the serial rights of *The Claverings* for the *Cornhill* for a sum which includes the right 'of disposing for their own advantage of the early sheets for America', and he grants them an option on the entire English and continental copyrights.

Trollope clearly for many years was content to leave his publishers to negotiate foreign arrangements 'for their own advantage'. He seems to have had no direct contact with Tauchnitz until 1872 when the *New York Morning Herald* announced that as a result of a lawsuit Trollope had extracted large damages from Tauchnitz for infringement of copyright. This was pure fabrication. One result was an exchange of letters between the two men. Trollope wrote:

> Latterly in order that I might avoid the trouble of many bargainings I have sold my novels with all the rights of copyright to the English purchaser, and have therefore given over to him the power of doing what he pleases as to foreign editions. . . . As to the future I will arrange that the German re-publication shall be with you. I am so fond of your series that I regret to have a work of mine omitted from it.

And in his agreements for *The Way We Live Now*, 1873, and *The Prime Minister*, 1874, there are clauses expressly debarring Chapman & Hall from 'selling the right of republication in Germany to any other firm than that of Baron Tauchnitz of Leipzig'. What remains mysterious is that, while the baron had published twenty-two books by Trollope before 1873 and was to publish more than as many thereafter, between 1873 and 1876 three of his Chapman & Hall novels (*The Eustace Diamonds*, *Miss Mackenzie* and *Phineas Redux*) were published on the continent by the rival firm, Asher of Berlin.

Caroline Norton inherited a Celtic temperament from her Sheridan forebears. She was an unhappy lady who had been driven by adversity to fight for her rights and for women's rights generally. Sometimes on impulse she campaigned for imagined rights. In 1851 she sold a three-decker outright to Henry Colburn, and in 1863 and 1867 she sold two other three-deckers to Colburn's successors, Hurst & Blackett. It was stipulated in at least one of these agreements that the publisher could dispose of the books in America 'and elsewhere'. The continental rights in all three novels were sold by the London publishers to Tauchnitz through the intermediary of Sydney Williams, of Williams & Norgate, Tauchnitz's London agents; and in 1868 Hurst & Blackett assigned the copyright in the third novel, *Old Sir Douglas*, to Macmillan's. Three years later, in October–November 1871, there was an animated correspondence in *The Times* about piracies and unauthorized editions in the United States, the colonies and Europe in the course of which, flailing around with a crusading abandon, Mrs. Norton accused Mrs. Henry Wood of having stolen the plot of *East Lynne* from a short story which she, Mrs. Norton, had contributed to an annual many years earlier. She also wrote:

> I pass over the publication abroad by Baron Tauchnitz of Leipzig, and Galignani in Paris, of works provokingly full in every page of errors of type and mistakes of sense in consequence of not venturing to communicate with pirated authors.

The Times in the next week printed letters from several authors and publishers denying that Tauchnitz was a pirate, and testifying to his probity, liberality and accurate printing. A letter from Williams explained that Tauchnitz had bought the continental rights in Mrs. Norton's books from her London publishers.

Tauchnitz wrote to Mrs. Norton offering to shew her his contracts and expressing regrets for any errors in her novels. (He might have added that the errors in his reprint of *Old Sir Douglas* were all in Macmillan's cheap edition, a fact of which Mrs. Norton had complained to Macmillan's three years before.) Mrs. Norton reading carelessly took Tauchnitz's letter as an apology for piracy and wrote to Williams to say so. She also wrote to Alexander Macmillan about Williams's 'impudent assertions' and 'unmitigated falsehoods' and publicly announced that she would prosecute him for libel. *The Times* decided to close the correspondence, 'which is becoming too heated for our columns. The controversy will be best conducted in the cool atmosphere of a court of law.' Some of Mrs. Norton's letters which I have been privileged to see in the Macmillan archives are plainly hysterical. In a calmer moment she admitted that she did not 'comprehend all these complicated arrangements', meaning the sale of copyrights, and she told Tauchnitz that she had not known of international copyright or known that he paid his English authors. One of her difficulties in dealing with controversial correspondence was absence from her documents. 'I am never in London at this time of year', she wrote to the baron. 'I go from Château to Château of friends in Scotland and England, making autumn and winter visits. . . . If I had known the truth about *you* and your good German heart. . . .' Other examples of the author–publisher relationship illustrate authors' dissatisfactions over fees, but I have yet to discover an instance in the nineteenth century of a dissatisfied author not being won back to happy relations with Tauchnitz and his good German heart.

In 1864 Tennyson wrote to Tauchnitz, 'With respect to my new volume, Messrs. Williams & Norgate write to me asking what sum I require for granting you permission to print it in Germany. I think I had better leave this matter entirely in your hands.' Four years later Tennyson evidently repented of having accepted Tauchnitz's offer, whatever that offer was. In a letter rather more gracious than the extract might suggest he wrote:

I am quite aware that I made rather a bad bargain with you, in selling the continental copyright for so small a sum, and my publisher affirms (whether rightly or not) that I annually lose some hundreds of pounds by this tran-saction. I am also aware that the royalty you offer me now is all of your free grace, and that I have no claim upon you.

Whether Tauchnitz offered a *royalty* as early as 1868 is doubt-ful: the poet laureate may have used the word inadvertently. Relations between poet and publisher remained cordial and Tennyson continued to entrust his continental rights to Tauch-nitz.

Then there is Stevenson. He was indignant at an offer of only £20 for *Treasure Island*, which indeed in retrospect seems very little; but the book was after all a 'juvenile' by a little-known writer and, as Tauchnitz said, 'rather a small book, filling only *one* of my cheap volumes'. 'Yon puir Tauchnitz (if that be his name)', Stevenson wrote to a friend, 'comes between me and my vivers. It's a dam shame, by what I can see—a fair disgrace—and him a common German. *Tauch*! says you. *Nitz*! says I, and gives ye them'. That was in April 1884. In July (fig. 9) having accepted the £20 Stevenson writes to the common German, 'I am pleased indeed to appear in your splendid collection, and thus to rise a grade in the hierarchy of my art.'

Twenty pounds was then, and for some years had been, an average price for the continental rights of a single-volume work by a little-known writer. Figures are scarce, but a few can be found. In 1865 the highest fee went to Carlyle, £225 for the last four volumes of *Frederick the Great*. Next comes Dinah Mulock (Mrs. Craik), at the height of her fame, with £50 each for two one-volume novels. Dickens gets an average of £37. 10s. a volume for *Our Mutual Friend*; Mrs. Henry Wood £30 a volume for *Oswald Cray*; Charles Lever only £30 for the two volumes of *Luttrell of Arran*. Lesser known writers fared worse: Mrs. Riddell and Annie Thomas only £12. 10s. a volume. In 1875–7 Gladstone was happy to accept £25 each for three volumes of political essays. In the eighties Macmillan's, apart from celebrities, regularly sold novels to Tauchnitz at about £20 or £30. If we consider that in 1892 Tauchnitz's rivals Heinemann & Balestier of Leipzig paid only 25 guineas to Gissing, an established if doubtfully popular author, for

VERTRAG

zwischen *Robert Louis Stevenson Esq., London*

und

Bernhard Freiherrn von Tauchnitz, Firma: Bernhard Tauchnitz

zu Leipzig.

§. 1.

Es überträgt *Robert Louis Stevenson Esq.*
an Herrn Frhrn. v. Tauchnitz das ausschliessliche Recht, das Werk:

" *Treasure Island* "

in englischer Sprache für den Continent zu verlegen.

§. 2.

Es macht sich Herr Frhr. v. Tauchnitz verbindlich in keiner Weise seine
Ausgaben des erwähnten Werkes nach England oder dessen Colonieen zu verkaufen.

§. 3.

Es zahlt Herr Frhr. v. Tauchnitz für Uebertragung dieses Verlagsrechtes
an *Robert Louis Stevenson Esq.* ein für allemal die Summe
von *Zwanzig Pfund Sterling (£ 20 Sterling)*

§. 4.

Dieser Vertrag ist in zwei gleichlautenden Exemplaren von beiden Theilen
vollzogen worden.

Leipzig *und London,*
den 12. Mai 1884.

Robert Louis Stevenson

FIG. 9. Tauchnitz contract for *Treasure Island*

Denzil Quarrier, then £20 for *Treasure Island* in 1884 does not seem so much of 'a dam shame'.

A single Tauchnitz volume was priced originally at half one Prussian Thaler (or dollar), which under the Empire became M. 1. 60, the equivalent of 2 francs in France or 1s. 6d. in Britain. On the continent the standard bookseller's discount was 50 per cent, but for bulk purchases Tauchnitz might have to allow even more. Bulk means in this context not a large number of copies of a particular title but a mixed bag of new and popular old books for, shall we say, Hachette to display on their railway bookstalls throughout France. (Hachette, besides being publishers and wholesale booksellers, had for many years the sort of monopoly of railway bookstalls in France that W. H. Smith used to enjoy in England.) How many copies Tauchnitz printed whether of long-selling novels like Dickens's or of short-lived novels like Annie Thomas's or of speculative newcomers like Stevenson is not known: but he must have reckoned that the assured sale of an average book lasted only about two years. A sale of 2,000 copies at 1s. 6d. represents a retail total of £150. If a trade discount of 50 per cent is allowed and supposing the author to be given a royalty of 10 per cent, the author gets £15 and the publisher is left with a total of £60 to cover production, advertisement, overheads and his own profit—not an excessive margin. If he had bought the continental copyright for £20 his margin on 2,000 copies was even smaller; if the book succeeded on the other hand over a long term of years he stood to make a fair, even a large profit.

Two writers whose financial dealings with Tauchnitz can be followed in detail are George Eliot and Mrs. Humphry Ward.† In 1858 George Eliot accepted £30 for the two volumes of her first work of fiction, *Scenes of Clerical Life*. Next year she refused the same sum for *Adam Bede*. Williams & Norgate told Blackwood, her Edinburgh publisher, that Tauchnitz in his anxiety to have the book would pay £50 if the author insisted. 'The impudence with

† George Eliot in Gordon S. Haight's fine edition of her letters, and Mrs. Ward in the papers which, since this lecture was given, have been acquired by the Honnold Library, Claremont.

which Williams & Norgate "try it on" for Tauchnitz', George Lewes wrote, 'is to me amazing.' For *The Mill on the Floss* in 1860 Williams & Norgate offered £80 but were forced up to £100—that is £50 a volume. In the mid-sixties George Eliot and Blackwood, like some other authors and publishers, came to question whether cheap continental editions did not injure the sale of ordinary English editions. At first they refused to allow *Felix Holt* to be published in Leipzig. Some months after *Felix Holt* had appeared in Britain, however, the author was in Paris. She found in 'society' there a 'deep regret' that the book was not in the Tauchnitz collection, 'the only medium by which the English text of English novels can get known on the continent'. Four years later Tauchnitz who hitherto had enjoyed a virtual monopoly on the continent found his supremacy challenged. In 1871 Albert Cohn of the Berlin firm of Asher inaugurated 'Asher's Collection of English and American Authors, Copyright Editions'. The very first volume in the new series was the first of eight volumes of George Eliot's *Middlemarch*. Asher's had agreed to pay the author a royalty, not a lump sum. 'I fancy we have done a good turn to English authors generally by setting off Asher's series', she wrote to Blackwood, 'for we have heard that Tauchnitz has raised his offers'; and a year later at Bad Homburg she observed that 'Asher's cheap editions are visible everywhere by the side of Tauchnitz, but their outside is not, I think, quite equally recommendable and recommending'.

The Asher collection, after a few years transferred from Berlin to the firm of Grädener & Richter in Hamburg, was a serious threat to Tauchnitz. It seduced from him in its first year Miss Braddon, Miss Broughton and Ouida. But its life was brief. In ten years it ran to only 200 volumes compared with nearly a thousand of Tauchnitz's in the same years. Miss Braddon, Miss Broughton and Ouida quickly returned to the baron; so with *Daniel Deronda* in 1876 did George Eliot. The early nineties saw the fall of the house of Asher: the Firma Tauchnitz stood firm for another fifty years.

The figure of 2,000 copies for an average, possibly ephemeral book in the 1860s to 1880s was arrived at not altogether at random.

Reliable evidence of the sale of one Tauchnitz book names a little more than twice that figure, but the book was a best-seller in two continents and the date is the early nineties. In roughly two years the sale of Mrs. Humphry Ward's *David Grieve*, 1892, amounted to about 80,000 copies in England, 60,000 copies in America, and in the colonies about 10,000 copies. Tauchnitz in the same period sold 4,400 at a loss. He had paid dearly for the copyright, £100 a volume, and would only break even, he told Mrs. Ward, if sales reached 5,000. Yet, as he wrote, 'after the elapse of $2\frac{1}{4}$ years the continuation of the sale is of no importance any more'—in other words sales had virtually stopped short of 4,500. Mrs. Ward was of the type of author whom publishers call 'greedy'. Though she knew that Tauchnitz was out of pocket over *David Grieve* she asked for her next novel, *Marcella*, either the same sum (£300) or £250 on advance of a 15 per cent royalty. The younger Tauchnitz, who like his father thought royalties quite unsuitable to cheap series and regarded 15 per cent as excessive, was able to point out to her that if she had had a 15 per cent royalty on *David Grieve* up to the time when sales fell off she would have received only £160 instead of the £300 which he had paid her. They compromised on £250 down for *Marcella*, with £50 more to come if 5,000 copies should be sold.

The fees for these two books were exceptional. In 1888 Tauchnitz had paid his usual £20 a volume for Mrs. Ward's *Robert Elsmere* which before its unforeseeable success he had thought unlikely to have any wide appeal on the continent; but he agreed in advance to make a further payment if sales warranted. He had done the same with J. H. Shorthouse's *John Inglesant*. In due course Mrs. Ward received an additional £30. But between *Robert Elsmere* in 1888 and *David Grieve* in 1892 Tauchnitz's dominance of the European market had again been threatened. In 1889–90 William Heinemann had set up two businesses: one in London which still bears his name, and the firm of Heinemann & Balestier in Leipzig (fig. 10). Balestier was a young American who died not long afterwards and whose sister was to marry Rudyard Kipling. Heinemann was an energetic young man whose family had come

LEIPZIG
BERLIN
VIENNA
PARIS

𝕮𝖍𝖊 𝕰𝖓𝖌𝖑𝖎𝖘𝖍 𝕷𝖎𝖇𝖗𝖆𝖗𝖞:

A COLLECTION OF THE

LATEST AND BEST WORKS OF FICTION AND GENERAL LITERATURE FOR CONTINENTAL READING.

June, 1891.

FIG. 10. Heinemann & Balestier catalogue

from Hanover and who quickly, by offering large advances on royalties, built up a strong list of fiction and general literature in London. For his Leipzig venture he relied partly on this list and partly on the purchase of continental rights from other publishers. As a result Tauchnitz was forced to pay higher prices to his authors than before, sometimes higher than sales were likely to justify. He paid them because he could not afford to lose his authors if he was, in the long run, to defeat his competitors. So much is implicit in his correspondence with Mrs. Ward. Nevertheless before the new century was five years old Heinemann had pulled out of Leipzig. The younger Tauchnitz, with nearly 4,000 volumes to his credit and more than a million stereotype plates in his armoury, was left in undisputed possession of the field.

I shall close my account of Tauchnitz with an example of a publisher's difficulty in understanding the intricacies of international copyright. It concerns Tauchnitz, Macmillan's and Tennyson. Macmillan's had always been jealous of all their rights, including the right to refuse or to charge a fee for permission for other publishers to reprint poems of which they held the copyright. They had registered certain of Tennyson's books in Paris and Berlin in order to protect their copyright in France and Germany and they sold their continental rights to Tauchnitz in competition with Hachette. Tauchnitz in 1885 gave Hachette licence to reprint certain poems of Tennyson's in a school text-book. Macmillan's were immediately up in arms. In a draft letter which seems not to have been posted they accused the baron of having acted from the base motive of conciliating a firm who were in a position to keep his books off the railway bookstalls. Tauchnitz's reply to the somewhat milder letter he received was that in France and Germany copyright was indivisible: he had bought the Tennyson continental copyrights, not a licence to print the poems solely in his collection of British authors. Moreover he had not charged Hachette anything because he was not interested in reprints of poems for school use, and he would gladly refrain from giving permissions in future if Macmillan's would refrain from selling on the continent their editions of books of which they themselves had sold Tauchnitz the continental rights. It had not occurred to Macmillan's until he pointed it out that they were acting as pirates on his ground. It had been the proud boast of the Firma Tauchnitz that from the earliest days of international copyright they had never sent one of their copyright British books to a British territory except at the request of the British copyright proprietor, which international law allowed.

IV

THE UNITED STATES BEFORE AND AFTER
1891

LET me begin with what Mr. Gladstone said in 1887. International copyright with America, he wrote to Alexander Macmillan, is 'a big subject, growing bigger and bigger *à vue d'oeil*, and likely, after two or three generations, to be bigger than it now is by five or six-fold'. The prophecy has been honoured in our own century.

I shall be looking at American law through the eyes of British authors and publishers, with illustrations drawn from celebrated Oxford men—Liddell and Scott of Christ Church; Gladstone, also of Christ Church; Jowett of Balliol; James Bryce of Trinity. All these writers (or in the case of the lexicographers their British publishers, the Clarendon Press) were alive to the implications of the first United States international copyright act, commonly called the 'Chace act', of 1891. These illustrations I owe in large part to the courtesy of the delegates of the Press; others to the courtesy of the directors of Macmillan & Company. If from time to time I seem to harp on Henry James it is because he was an American writer domiciled in Britain and published by Macmillan's in both countries: it is eight years since I suggested in an article on collecting James that his books 'provide almost a skeleton history of inter-continental copyright and piracy in the late nineteenth century'. Moreover his books are readily accessible if not all in Bodley at least not far away.

First a few words about some of the requirements of American law before the Chace act. One such requirement was registration of a book by deposit of the title-page before publication. Another was the deposit of a copy or copies of the book itself within a stated period after publication—within six months up to 1831; three months between 1831 and 1865; one month between 1865 and 1870; and ten days up to 1891. These periods are now of interest mainly to those who seek to determine precise priorities to the nearest day of publication as between American and British first editions: such persons, bibliographers or collectors, must beware of confusing either the date of registration of title or that of deposit of copy with the actual publication date. At the time however such matters were of vital importance to the British publisher if the book he was to copyright in Britain was also to be copyright by an American author or publisher in the United States. Under British law the 'world première', so to speak, must be the British edition. The necessary sequence therefore—in say the 1880s—was (1) deposit of title-page in Washington; (2) publication of book in Britain; (3) American publication, and deposit of copies within ten days; (4) deposit in the British Museum within a month of (2); with (5) optional registration at Stationers' Hall at any time after (2) if the British publisher sought to maintain his rights in the courts. (You could not register in Britain *before* publication, because copyright was only brought into existence *by* publication.) This sequence meant a tight schedule for the two publishers, British and American. The slightest delay at the printers or binders or in the transit of sheets across the Atlantic might upset the sequence and imperil copyright. If the dates of publication in Dr. Blanck's *Bibliography of American Literature* are to be trusted—and he is hard to fault—many books by American authors sheltered under a protection in one country or the other to which they were not strictly entitled.

This situation was aggravated by the Chace act which required deposit in Washington of an American-printed edition 'on or before the day of publication in this or any foreign country'. In other words to conform with both United States and British law a book must be published in both countries simultaneously. Publishers on both sides of the Atlantic found this requirement virtually impossible to meet, and in 1909 a further American act (*Statutes at Large*, xxxv (1909), 1075–88) gave notable relief. Thereafter an English-language work printed outside the United States if deposited in Washington within thirty days of first publication abroad was granted *ad interim* copyright for another thirty days, within which period full copyright could be secured by manufacture of an authorized edition in the United States.

Another requirement of American law was that a notice should appear in the book in the form 'Entered according to act of Congress, in the year ——, by A. B., in the clerk's office of' such-and-such a district court, or from 1870 'in the office of the Librarian of Congress, at Washington'. From 1874 it was enough to print simply 'Copyright, 1874, by A. B.'. Before the Chace act there was no law requiring a book to be of American manufacture: many books by American authors were type-set in Britain and either plates or printed sheets were shipped to the United States. No copyright notice was required under British law, but if a printer was not careful copies prepared for the British market without the American copyright notice on the title-verso might go to the States. Macmillan's in 1886 instructed their Edinburgh printers to print a title-page of Henry James's *The Bostonians* for deposit at Washington before publication with the copyright notice on the verso. A few days later they discovered that the title-versos of the completed book did not carry the notice in the prescribed form and cancels of the two preliminary leaves had to be printed.

The west–east complement of this situation arises not out of copyright legislation but out of customs and merchandise marks acts. An American publisher selling sheets to a British publisher with the latter's imprint on the title-page had to remember to instruct his printer to insert, what United States law did not demand, the printer's name and place of business: if that place of business shared a name with a British town the state or country of origin must be added—New York was enough, Cambridge was not. If there were no indication of foreign origin the words 'London: Chapman & Hall' would be tantamount to a 'mark' signifying that the merchandise was of British manufacture; and since it was not, the customs officers ever alert would declare the import of the sheets illegal.

In the same year that Macmillan's had to print cancels for *The Bostonians* they published another three-decker by Henry James, *The Princess Casamassima*. They made stereotypes for a one-volume edition and printed sheets for America. When the time came to publish a one-volume English edition they still had sheets with '1886' on the title-page and ordered cancels dated '1887', taking advantage of this cancellation to add the legend 'All rights reserved'. I must pause for a moment over this phrase 'All rights reserved'. Soon after they had published the first volumes of their English Men of Letters series in 1878 Macmillan's offered the translation rights to a German publisher. The publisher blandly replied that Macmillan's had no translation rights because they had failed to print a notice reserving such rights on the title-pages of the original editions. Only then did Macmillan's look up a twenty-seven-year-old act of parliament to discover that reservation of rights of translation must be notified on title-pages. This was the act of 1852, passed primarily to give effect to the Anglo-French copyright convention. The form of words was not specified in the act, but after the case of *Cassell* v. *Stiff* in 1856 it appears to have been assumed that the words 'The right of reproduction is reserved' were sufficient to cover both dramatization and translation.† In 1886 the section in the act requiring such a notice in books was repealed, but not the section requiring it in periodicals.

In the United States it was not until 1870 that authors were enabled by statute to 'reserve the right to dramatize or to translate their own works' (*Statutes at Large*, xvi (1871), 212). An official regulation under the statute specified that the words 'Right of

---

† One issue in *Cassell* v. *Stiff* was argued under 15 & 16 Vict. c. 12, s. 7. This protected the author of a non-political article in a foreign periodical provided he had 'signified his intention of preserving [*sic*] the copyright therein, and the right of translating the same'. The case concerned the piracy of illustrations and their descriptions which had first appeared in the Paris *L'Illustration*, and the judge held that 'a notice that the plaintiff reserves his right of "reproduction"' was 'a sufficiently apt word in this case'. Section 8 of the act dealt with translations of books and dramatic pieces to which, on a layman's view, 'reproduction' seems less apt.

The word 'reproducing' is used once in the first act (25 & 26 Vict. c. 68 (1862)) to create copyright in paintings, drawings and photographs, but 'reproduction' does not appear in any act concerned with book copyright before the Berne convention of which the English text is a translation from the French. Nevertheless British publishers commonly printed on their title-pages of unillustrated books in the 60s–80s the caveat 'The right of translation and reproduction is reserved'. I suspect that they or their legal advisers confused 'reproduction' (loosely meaning 'reprinting') with 'representation' (of dramatic pieces based on their texts). 'All rights reserved' was a safer phrase.

translation reserved' or 'All rights reserved' must be printed 'below the notice of copyright entry'—that is, with normal books, on the title-verso. So a publisher if he was to conform strictly to the laws of both countries must in theory put the words 'All rights reserved' (or their equivalent) on his British title-page and on his American title-verso. No wonder from time to time publishers nodded.

Most of the countries of Europe adopted in or soon after 1887 the Berne copyright convention. The British parliament had passed an act the year before empowering the Queen to do so by order in council. The convention established a Copyright Union (in the words of the preamble) 'for protecting effectually and in as uniform a manner as possible the rights of authors over their literary and artistic works'. This was the end of a long stretch of uphill road beset with obstacles which copyright reformers had wearily traversed for half a century. That it was not the true end of the road was due to the protectionist policy of the United States. The States did not adopt the Berne convention. The Chace act four years later empowered the president by proclamation to extend copyright protection to citizens or subjects of foreign states provided those states permitted to American citizens 'the benefit of copyright on substantially the same basis as its own citizens'. What the act did not do was to grant American protection to aliens on anything like the same basis as was enjoyed by nationals of the Berne convention states. That convention made no stipulation about where a book should be printed. The Chace act required books if they were to secure American copyright to be printed from type set in the United States or from plates made from such type. This was a concession to the American typographical unions who foretold utter ruin if copyright editions of foreign authors' books could be printed abroad for import into America.

One part of this fear was that if British authors' books could be copyright in America even when printed abroad the copies exported to America, where unauthorized reprinting would no longer be legal, would be much more expensive than America was accustomed to. American booksellers foresaw that they would have to handle the traditional English three-decker, but as Frederick Macmillan wrote to Marion Crawford, 'English publishers are not such fools as to try anything of the sort; and if they were, English authors would not submit to having their books offered for sale in the U.S. in an unacceptable shape'. At one point it was suggested that to get round this the United States should put a prohibitive duty on expensive books and admit cheap books free of duty. Obviously the American printer would not accept this.

Macmillan believed that the manufacture clause in the Chace bill was supported by American publishers and printers because

it would put the entire manufacture of books for the English-speaking world in their hands. They argue that, as a book could only be copyright in America on condition that it was printed there, while the same rule does not apply in England, it would be easy for them to purchase the entire right of producing an English book—to print it in America so as to obtain American copyright, and to ship over a certain number of copies to England (where there is no import duty) in order to supply the English market.

The real objections to the 'Chace bill' are (1) that it would lead to a great waste of money, as many authors would be tempted to go to the expense of having their books reprinted in the United States in order to secure an American copyright that might often turn out to be worthless; (2) authors might sometimes be driven to accept inadequate terms from American publishers rather than risk the loss of the American copyright altogether; and (3) in many instances (particularly in the case of first books by unknown writers) the copyright which might afterwards turn out to be valuable would be lost because an author without means of his own had been unable to find an American publisher prepared to risk the money necessary for a reprint.

I would not have you think that I have got my British bull-dog teeth into protectionist Uncle Sam. There was enlightenment as well as self-interest on both sides. From the late 1830s onwards many American authors, publishers and politicians worked as hard for truly reciprocal international copyright as did British. Between 1843, the year of Dickens's first visit to America when he talked of little else, and 1886, the year before the Berne convention, no fewer than eleven international copyright bills were presented to the United States Congress only to fall by the wayside. A twelfth bill, Senator Chace's, hung fire until 1890; his name survives because the thirteenth bill, an unlucky thirteenth compromise between enlightenment and protectionism, signed by President Harrison in 1891, was substantially the same as Senator Chace's had been.†

In the United States in the hundred years before 1891 only a citizen or resident could acquire copyright in a printed book. But there were methods by which a foreigner might seek to get round the law. One of these was by residing in the United States, as Captain Marryat did for an extended stay in 1838; but when Marryat tested his rights in the courts it was decided against him that 'resident' implied a declared intention to become a citizen and the idea of renouncing allegiance to his Queen was abhorrent to a Captain, R.N., retired. Another method of evading the spirit of the law, while observing the letter, was to write your book in collaboration with an American citizen and have it entered in his name. On one occasion an American publisher suggested that Kipling should find an American collaborator. This collaborator

> might indeed be only a hack writer, whose name would be of use simply on account of its carrying the copyright. . . . I believe it to be quite possible to copyright a book in this country, only one or two of the stories in which are by an American author, and without stating which author is responsible for a designated story.

Kipling refused, perhaps because he would not imperil his literary integrity.

Neither T. H. Huxley nor James Bryce had such scruples. In 1866 apropos of his *Lessons in Elementary Physiology* Huxley wrote to Alexander Macmillan:

> I had a young Yankee friend [William Jay Youmans] working with me all last winter, and I have arranged with him to bring out an edition of my book with additions by him which will make it our joint property. Otherwise the thing would be pillaged at once.

Bryce's *Holy Roman Empire*, originally the Arnold prize essay for 1863, was widely pirated in America. Many years later he con-

---

† Honour where honour is due. In *The Question of Copyright*, New York, 1896, G. H. Putnam, secretary of the American Publishers' Copyright League, calls the act 'the Chace–Breckinridge–Adams–Simonds–Platt Copyright Act'.

sidered allowing an American scholar to annotate a school edition simply in order that it should qualify for copyright. Bryce would have preferred to annotate it himself, and indeed he did so after the act of 1891 when he could himself secure copyright in a revised edition. More important, with the same copyright end in view Bryce having consulted Judge Oliver Wendell Holmes arranged for certain chapters in his book on the *American Commonwealth*, 1888, a book of such scope and originality that it was bound to attract the pirates, to be written by American specialists. These chapters were offprinted as pamphlets and copyrighted in Washington and London and one or two copies were exposed for sale in order to effect publication. But Bryce's 'plan to defeat the pirates', as he called it, miscarried.† It was open to any American publisher to reprint the greater part of the book omitting the copyright chapters. One publisher did so. After the Chace act Bryce sufficiently revised the book to ensure United States copyright for his third edition; but the competitive sale of the cheap piracy of the earlier text promised to be so damaging that Macmillan's yielding to blackmail bought and destroyed the pirate's stereotype plates. (A curious complication arose out of Bryce's book when a libel action was brought against him over one of the chapters he had not himself written. That is another story.)

That great undertaking of the Clarendon Press, Liddell & Scott's *Greek-English Lexicon*, enjoyed British copyright in its various editions and revisions from its first appearance in 1843. To the seventh edition, 1882, three American professors made extensive contributions spread throughout the work. As American citizens they assigned their rights to Harpers, the New York publishers, who proceeded to register the copyright in the whole work in America. Liddell & Scott did not in 1882 have to be printed in

---

† Among the more important attempts to 'defeat the pirates' by incorporating contributions by American writers in a substantially British work were four actions brought by A. & C. Black of Edinburgh between 1879 and 1890 against unauthorized publishers of the *Encyclopaedia Britannica*. Black's lost their first action but had the satisfaction of seeing their rivals lose money by the piracy and go out of business. The later suits were decided in Black's favour, but not until after the Chace bill had modified the climate of public and legal opinion.

America, but its status after the Chace act was uncertain. In 1891 Harper's two-dollar abridged edition was pirated in a photographic reproduction at $1.25. Harpers decided not to test their claim in the courts but to undercut the piracy by printing in America from Clarendon Press electros and by publishing at $1.00 even though this meant publishing at a loss. This was questionably legitimate: for though the book was printed in the States the type had not been set there. Ten years later in 1901 Liddell & Scott was the subject of a significant United States Treasury decision. Harpers had assigned their copyright in the seventh edition to the American Book Company. The company sought to import sheets of the further revised eighth edition, 1897, from England only to find their consignment detained by the United States customs as a violation of the Chace act. The United States Treasury, adopting the opinion of the attorney-general, decided in the company's favour on the grounds that the act was not retrospective ('a law speaks from the date of its approval'); that American copyrights registered before 1891 remained valid; that books copyright before 1891 could still be imported from abroad; and that as the revisions of 1897 were not 'substantial' no new registration of copyright was necessary.

The next relevant United States Treasury decision on book copyright, in 1903, cleared up another point. The phrase in the Chace act, 'printed from type set within the limits of the United States, or from plates made therefrom', might appear to imply not only type-setting but machining in the States. It was now so interpreted that if the type had been set and the plates made in the States copies printed abroad from those plates for the proprietor of the copyright could lawfully be imported into America without violation of the statute. This loop-hole in the protectionist bastion however was closed by the United States act of 1909.

Unlike Bryce and Liddell & Scott, Dr. Jowett had no means of securing United States copyright in his translation of the *Dialogues of Plato*: one somehow cannot imagine him inviting American professors to supply the scholarly introductions and analyses. The Clarendon Press editions marketed in America in the 1870s were copied by unauthorized publishers and Master Jowett resented what he held to be piracy. In the late eighties when it had become clear that if the Congress should pass an international copyright act one of the conditions would be manufacture in America Jowett set about revising his *Plato*. He suggested to the delegates that the revised edition should be printed in America after the act should have been passed. Yet even after the act had been passed in March 1891 with effect from the following 1 July there remained another hurdle to be taken. Would the president regard British law as at that time in force, in effect the Berne convention, as satisfying the condition of giving United States citizens substantially the same protection in Britain as British citizens themselves enjoyed? According to Edward Marston, the publisher-expert on copyright law, writing that spring to her Majesty's minister at Washington, many contracts had been entered into by publishers and authors in the full expectation that the president would immediately utter the necessary proclamation in favour of Britain. But though satisfied with existing American privilege under French law the president was believed to have doubts about British. Legislation might be necessary at Westminster to bring British law into line: Lord Monkswell was preparing a bill.

An entry in the 'Orders of the Delegates of the Press' for 19 June 1891 reads:

> With reference to the American Copyright Act:
>
> Various communications from Lord Monkswell, Mr John Murray, Messrs Macmillan & Co., and Mr Peter Williams† were reported, pointing out that no rights could be acquired by English Authors in America under the new Copyright Act until the issue of a proclamation by the President of the United States declaring that the English Law of Copyright satisfies the conditions of Section 13 of the American Act. . . .
>
> It was resolved that in the event of the President of the United States issuing the needful proclamation under Section 13, the Secretary shall take the necessary steps to obtain American Copyright for the new edition of Jowett's *Dialogues of Plato*, arranging to print an edition in America, and to sell copies to Messrs Macmillan & Co., or some other firm.

† Macmillan's were New York agents for the Clarendon Press. Williams was the Press's legal adviser.

It was further resolved to decline the offer of Messrs Macmillan & Co. to undertake the cost of printing an edition of this work in America, paying a royalty of ten per cent if the book acquires copyright, but nothing if it is pirated.

The president signed his first proclamation under the act on the earliest possible day, covering among others France, Great Britain and the British possessions. Lord Monkswell's bill was dropped. Jowett, having insisted that his work should be 'a fine specimen of American typography, in a form best suited to the American public' with 'a well proportioned page with a good margin', made his choice from a number of specimen pages submitted to him. The work was entered at Washington in the following February and the five volumes were duly published at $20.00. This should have meant the end of piracy, and indeed the 1892 edition was secure. But it is not the end of the story. One Professor Gardner of Smith College, Northampton, Massachusetts, complained to the publishers of the price. He could afford $20.00 himself but his students could not; and in view of 'the ever-increasing interest in philosophical studies in this country', he wrote, it ought to be possible to produce something cheaper—his students had to be satisfied with what he called the 'old badly printed edition'. This was an unauthorized reprint of the 1871 edition still being printed from twenty-year-old plates; its continuance, as their New York agents wrote to the Press, was still hampering the sale of the revised edition a year after the latter had secured copyright.

There are one or two points in the extract from the orders of the delegates which call for comment. First there is Macmillan's suggestion that they should pay a royalty if the *Plato* secured copyright but nothing if it should be pirated. It had long been common form for those American publishers who made gratuitous payments to British authors for their books—and several did so even though the books could not be copyright—to insert a clause in their contracts to the effect that in the event of an unauthorized reprint appearing the royalty would cease. Secondly the need to await the presidential proclamation. This had a special importance for publishers of plays. Henry Arthur Jones was particularly anxious that his play *Saints and Sinners* should be one of the first books to take advantage of the new American law. But if he was precipitate and his publishers went ahead before the proclamation the consequences for Jones would be disastrous. He would not only acquire no book copyright; he would also lose the even more valuable stage-rights which United States law gave to the unpublished plays even of foreign playwrights. On the other hand there were circumstances in which it was in a publisher's interest not to await but to anticipate the proclamation. Fisher Unwin had a book by the American author J. J. Roche at the printers in England late in June. If he could enter it at Washington before 1 July he could claim copyright for an edition printed in England: if not, he was faced with the choice of resetting in the United States or of forfeiting United States copyright.

Jowett and Jones were by no means alone in seeking to take advantage of the Chace act. All British authors stood to gain for the first time from American sales. Many, Bryce among them, immediately demanded higher royalties than either British or American publishers—the latter gratuitously—had been willing to pay in the face of threats of cheap unauthorized rival editions. If the justification of higher royalties was the removal of the fear of piracy, however, such royalties must increase the price of books and this was precisely what British publishers had assured the American trade would not result from international copyright agreement. British publishers, including several who had not operated in the United States before, hoped greatly to extend their markets, but they were faced with the American publishers' similar hope of invading the British market—bidding high, that is, not only for the American but for the 'world' rights in books by successful British writers. Just as Tauchnitz stepped up his fees when threatened by rival firms on the continent so now British publishers if they were to compete with American rivals were driven for a time at least to offer higher, sometimes uneconomic, advances to their own authors. Apropos of Tauchnitz I spoke of Mrs. Humphry Ward as a 'greedy' author. She was certainly a shrewd business woman. Moreover in 1890 she wanted to buy a country house.

Emboldened by the success of *Robert Elsmere* (a Macmillan book in America, though widely pirated), and while it was still uncertain whether the Congress would pass the Chace bill, she asked Scribner's for the unprecedented sum of £7,000 for advance proofs—she had no United States copyright to offer them—of her next novel *David Grieve*. Scribner's came back with an offer of £1,500, later increased to £2,250, which her London publisher George Smith of Smith, Elder advised her to accept without further bargaining lest it were withdrawn. One sunny morning in June 1891 Smith met Frederick Macmillan riding in the park on the way to work. Macmillan there and then offered £7,000 'for the entire American copyright (including Canadian) of Mrs. Ward's new novel'. This was accepted on the same day and three days later Smith wrote to Mrs. Ward:

> I do not think that Messrs Macmillan & Co. expect to make a profit from your book. The inducement to them was found in the idea that, at this juncture, it would be a good move on their part to do a noticeable transaction which would shew English authors and the world at large that they were able to compete successfully with American publishers.

Macmillan's New York manager commented:

> I am not at all sorry to hear that you have bought Mrs. Ward's novel, notwithstanding the enormous sum asked for it, for while I cannot think that the venture will shew a money profit, the gain indirectly should prove very great and the publication of this book should have a decidedly good effect on the remainder of the list.

Mrs. Ward bought her country house. Several years later Macmillan's of New York were still wistfully hoping to recoup through her later novels some of the loss they had suffered on *David Grieve*.

I said I would make one of my points from Gladstone. I do so without disrespect. In 1895 the secretary of the Clarendon Press wrote to their New York agent apropos of *Studies Subsidiary to the Works of Bishop Butler*, 'Gladstone is very anxious to secure American copyright, to which in this case we should not attach as much importance as he does'. The point here is that in many instances where the risk of unauthorized reprints was small the advantage of

American copyright was offset by the saving in cost of printing a book in Britain and exporting sheets. As the secretary to the Press wrote to William Stebbing, of Worcester College and *The Times* newspaper, whose life of Raleigh was on the stocks,

> I must remind you that printing in America is more expensive than in England; that piratical publishing has accustomed Americans to buy books at a price which excludes remuneration to the author; and that if we reprint your book in America we shall either have to forgo profit, or issue it at a price which will possibly choke off buyers.
>
> On the other hand if we do not reprint the book in America, we shall probably sell 500 copies of our English edition there—not at the full price, but at prices which will show a profit, and without risk.

It might be supposed that the cost of book production had little to do with international copyright. But clearly a British publisher had to calculate costs, freight charges, insurance and import duty before deciding whether the American international copyright act was in any way beneficial to a particular book. He also had to take account of less tangible matters. When Jowett spoke of 'the form best suited to the American public' he was nearer the heart of the matter than he perhaps knew. The Americans were accustomed to paper which weight for weight was of less bulk than British paper. American taste demanded books with trimmed edges at a time when high-class British books were always untrimmed. The heat of the American sun caused some British bindings to fade more quickly than they did in our more temperate climate: blue cloths were especially vulnerable. When as a result of the Chace act a publisher weighed up the advantages of printing and binding in one country or the other all these points had to be considered.

To take first the seemingly trivial matter of the American sun, I would throw out two tidbits to any prospective historian of what we now call a 'dust-jacket'. It was in the context of fading bindings that Macmillan's in London decided in 1891 'that all books sent to America shall in future be protected by paper wrappers. Books published in smooth cloth will have printed paper wrappers as hitherto: books in rough cloth will be wrappered in white.'

The other tidbit is of earlier date. In 1886 apropos of a cheap edition which was to appear both in cloth and as what we now call a 'paperback' a confusion occurred between Macmillan's and their printers over the use of the word 'wrapper'. Macmillan's wrote, '*We* call it a *wrapper* when used as a cover attached to the book, and an *envelope* when it is detached.'

American book production in the nineties—I am speaking not of cheap reprints but of books of good quality—was more expensive than British because American compositors and proof-readers were paid higher wages. Paper was cheaper per lb.; but owing to restrictions on the import of esparto (designed to protect the American pulp trade) it was both heavier in relation to its bulk and of poorer quality. The manufacture of plates was cheaper and better. The custom of the American trade was to set the type; to make stereos, or more often electros, immediately after correction; and then having distributed the type to print from the plates. It was unusual for ink to come into contact with type after the final revise had been passed and some printers would not keep type standing for more than four weeks without a prohibitive rental. British publishers tended to export stereos, which good-class American printers disliked because they lacked the sharpness of electros; and as stereos required more time to make ready and more attention on the press the printers charged up to twice as much for printing from them. It might be found by anyone who searched the records that several British printers having become aware of this American preference imported American electrotyping plant in the early nineties, as R. & R. Clark of Edinburgh certainly did. The poorer quality of British stereos was less important at home where the normal practice was to print from type in the first instance; to keep type standing for immediate reprints; to make moulds if future sales were uncertain; and only to plate when exceptionally long runs were necessary or reprints over several years expected.†

---

† The British printer was not altogether enamoured of stereos. I am told by Mr. P. J. W. Kilpatrick of T. & A. Constable that at one time his firm when instructed to print a book from stereos would use electros for the prelims, without passing on the extra cost to the publishers, in order to achieve a more creditable 'shop window'.

Sometimes if a novel had to appear simultaneously in both countries the British printer would make plates from the single-volume
setting for America before leading out for the English three-
decker. After 1891 inevitably more books for the British market
were type-set in America for export either as plates or in sheets.
British taste did not like American paper any more than it liked
American spelling—what Frederick Macmillan called 'Websterian
monstrosities'. If British taste was to be satisfied British paper must
be exported to America, in spite of a 20 per cent import duty, for
printing books that would be exported back to Britain. Hence we
find British paper manufacturers such as Dickinson's sending out
representatives to the United States in 1891 and setting up agencies
there soon afterwards.

Besides its different constituents and bulk American paper was
made in different sizes from British. An ordinary crown octavo
English novel was printed on quad crown paper measuring 30 by
40 inches: each sheet produced four signatures in eights with a
page-size untrimmed of 7½ by 5 inches. The corresponding paper-
size in America was 'broad twelves', 23 × 41 inches, yielding two
duodecimo signatures of slightly larger dimensions before trimming: when trimmed the page-size was virtually the same as a
British novel. A traditional American printer would adjust his
margins to the size of his full sheet with the result that, given the
same type-area, the margins in the back of a book on American
paper would be wider than on British or British-style American-
made paper: with books printed before 1891 from two sets of
plates, an English edition printed in Britain and an American in
America, the variation in margin is not uncommon. A traditional
British publisher with an eye to a well proportioned page when
ordering a book for both markets might require his printer to
impose for untrimmed edges for the one and to reimpose for
trimmed edges (in effect to substitute wider furniture in the back-
margin gutters) for the other. Macmillan's even considered going
to this expense for their designedly cheap Colonial Library in 1886
—for the colonies also preferred trimmed edges. That they did not
do so was due not so much to a wish to save cost as to a decision

to run off colonial sheets for binding up in batches, according to demand, either trimmed in cloth or untrimmed (for the purchaser to bind if he wished) in wrappers.

Some of these points can be illustrated from books by Henry James. Two sets of plates of *The Portrait of a Lady* were cast in London, one for the first American edition, printed in Cambridge, Massachusetts, in 1881, and the other for the first one-volume English edition, printed in London in 1882:† the American trimmed and English untrimmed pages are of almost identical size, but the margins in the back are appreciably different. In the years immediately before the Chace act we have *The Bostonians* and *The Princess Casamassima*, 1886, *The Reverberator* and *The Aspern Papers*, 1888, and *A London Life*, 1889, all printed in London or Edinburgh and published by Macmillan's in two or three volumes in London and simultaneously in one volume in New York. The New York single volumes are substantially the same as the single volumes published in London some months later, but they are never precisely the same. Among other distinguishing marks there may be the date, if the New York/London interval ran from one calendar year to another (*Casamassima*); or information on a title-verso (*Aspern*); or integral advertisements with sterling substituted for dollar prices (*London Life*); or the binding if sheets and not bound copies were exported (*Reverberator*); or again the binding even when manufactured in Britain (*Bostonians*). (The first binding of *The Bostonians* was judged ugly and in bad taste by American booksellers and in response to an urgent appeal from their New York house Macmillan's adopted another for later consignments.) Because of the American distaste for untrimmed edges New York copies of *The Princess Casamassima*, 1886, have all edges trimmed: London copies, 1887, printed on the same paper and bound at the same bindery do not.‡

† Although these were 'duplicate plates' made from a single setting of type (the three-volume setting with the leads removed) they exhibit a number of textual variants.

‡ Owing to the poor sale of James's books at this time sheets of some of them remained at the printers for anything up to twenty years. It is evident that the distinctions noted were liable to be overlooked when sheets were bound up for later issue in one country or the other.

After the Chace act James's *The Lesson of the Master*, 1892, and *The Real Thing*, 1893, were printed in Boston for publication by Macmillan's in both New York and London. James's bibliographers describe the English 'issues' of both books as 'consisting of sheets of the first American edition' but this needs qualification. It is true that they were printed from the same plates by the same printer: so were colonial editions. But the differences are striking. The American impression of *The Lesson of the Master*, in which in the eccentric nineteenth-century American manner the signatures fall on the fourth instead of the first leaf of each gathering merely because the fourth recto happened to be page 17 or 33 or any other multiple of 16 plus 1, is printed on standard American paper; the impression for London imposed so that the signatures fall conventionally on each first leaf is printed on an American paper made to English specifications. The difference in the impositions can be seen clearly in the narrower back margins of the London edition (shown in frontispiece). But there is a more striking difference still. In American presswork the custom had persisted through the years of so placing the points on the tympan to secure correct register that the holes made in the paper by the spurs remained visible in the bolt at the head of the folded quire. Up to the early nineteenth century before books were cased in cloth, when in fact the book-buyer was expected to send his books to his own binder for trimming and binding, this was a common and unobjectionable practice: in America in the 1890s since the bolt was intended to be trimmed before casing there was still no harm. With the London edition of *The Lesson of the Master*, intended to be published with untrimmed edges, the point-holes are a visible blemish: later books printed by the same printer are free of this fault—an indirect effect perhaps of the Chace act on American printing practice. With *The Real Thing* in the following year Macmillan's decided on British paper for their London edition. It weighed 120 lbs. to the quad ream. So did the American paper for the New York edition: this, conforming to American taste, was less bulky on my reckoning by some 6 per cent. The colonial edition was on a cheaper 90 lb. paper. So you can see that there is cause to demur to Edel and Laurence's assertion that the London 'issue' of these two books consisted of 'sheets of the first American edition'.

Of these books of James's it should be observed that all those printed in Britain before 1891 had British editions in two or three volumes whereas those printed in the United States after 1891 did not. The decline of the three-decker from the mid-eighties until its death in the mid-nineties is well known to have resulted from domestic differences between British publishers, booksellers, circulating libraries and the Authors' Society. But it is not altogether fanciful to detect a contributory cause in American copyright law. After 1891 the British publisher was naturally reluctant to go to the expense of printing three volumes at home of a novel which had also to be manufactured as a single volume in America.

So far I have been talking glibly about 'books'—as though we all know what a book is. It has been easier so. But a 'book' is not always the simple work of one writer or even of one copyright proprietor. Legislators had to legislate for books of multiple authorship such as encyclopaedias; for abridgments, dramatizations and translations; for works first delivered orally such as lectures and sermons; and moreover for contributions to periodicals such as a serialized novel later published as a 'book' or articles or short stories first printed in a variety of periodicals and later collected into a 'book'. The laws of all countries had to be framed to cover all these and other complications. I shall deal only, and briefly, with periodicals. How did the elaborate time sequence previously described—registration, publication and deposit in America, publication, deposit and registration in Britain—apply in the case of a serialized novel or a collection of stories or essays?

I mentioned earlier Washington Irving's *Sketch Book*, 1819–20, parts of which were published in America before, and parts after, the publication of the whole in Britain. Registration gave Irving protection in America, but the parts not first published in Britain could not secure British protection. By the latter part of the century when magazines on both sides of the Atlantic were fiercely competing for serials by the most popular writers the problem had become complex indeed. The example I propose to give, Henry James's *A Portrait of a Lady*, rests on the assumption— which is something of an over-simplification—that provided an American's novel was entered at Washington before publication and provided the instalments appeared in Britain before they had appeared in America, copyright in the 1880s could be secured in both countries. It was necessary also in order to secure copyright in America that each periodical instalment or short story or article should carry the assertion that it was copyright: in Britain it must carry 'conspicuously' a claim to reservation of rights.

In 1879 Henry James was negotiating with Macmillan's the publication of *A Portrait of a Lady* in *Macmillan's Magazine*. He had already arranged for its appearance in the *Atlantic Monthly*. The editor of the *Atlantic*, William Dean Howells, disliked the idea of the publication of a serial in a London magazine at the same time as in his own Boston magazine because the London magazine competed with his in the American market. But as he was himself negotiating with James's help for one of his own novels to appear simultaneously in the *Atlantic* and in the *Cornhill* he could not seriously object. It was agreed between James and the two maga- zine editors that *A Portrait of a Lady* should start in *Macmillan's* in October 1880 and in the *Atlantic* in November 1880. This would give the monthly instalments British copyright by prior publica- tion. Nevertheless a complication soon arose. Copies of *Mac- millan's* reached America and reviews of Henry James's instalments appeared in American newspapers before subscribers to the *Atlantic* had received the issues containing those instalments. This Messrs. Houghton, Mifflin, publishers of the *Atlantic*, naturally dis- liked. Yet if the instalments of the novel had been printed in the two magazines in issues bearing the same date James would have risked his British copyright because *Macmillan's* always appeared on the first day of its stated month and the *Atlantic* on the fifteenth day of the previous month. Here again I suspect that many serialized novels nominally published simultaneously in British and American magazines failed to observe the British law of prior publication. The risk was greater if the novel was only to be serialized in an American periodical and started there several months before book publication in Britain. It was to avoid risks of this kind that American writers like Howells and Marion Crawford caused special copyright editions of half-a-dozen copies or so of some of their books, or at least of the early instalments, to be deposited in British copyright libraries in good time. One such copyright edition, Henry James's *The Ambassadors*, is only known to survive in the Cambridge University Library and the Bodleian.

V

COLONIAL PROBLEMS: CONCLUSION

English-speaking people seem destined to cover a large proportion of the world, and the market is, therefore, immense. The result ought to be that the remuneration of the English authors should be largely increased, and that the price of English books should be much diminished.

Thus Mr. Farrer (later Lord Farrer), permanent secretary to the board of trade, arguing before the royal commission in 1877 in favour of a single, unified imperial copyright. John Murray in the 1840s had failed in his enlightened attempt to supply the reading needs of the North American backwoods and India's remote cantonments. By the latter part of the century copyright and publishing in the empire had become matters not so much of complexity as of chaos. If I say that I do not know what the law was at any particular date I must not be charged with lack of curiosity or application. The royal commission annexed to their report a digest by Sir James Stephen which, they said, 'we believe to be a correct statement of the law as it stands'. Among other dubieties of the law as it stood Sir James posed the colonial problem:

> It is uncertain whether an author obtains copyright by publishing a book in the United Kingdom, after a previous publication thereof in parts of Her Majesty's dominions out of the United Kingdom.
> It is uncertain whether an author acquires copyright ... in any part of Her Majesty's dominions out of the United Kingdom (apart from any local law as to copyright which may be in force there) by the publication of a book in such part of Her Majesty's dominions.

It is hardly suprising that even where the law was moderately clear it was abused by those to whom abuse was profitable and often tacitly, sometimes avowedly, ignored by those whose duty it was to enforce it.

The 'colonies', to use the most convenient general term, were as varied in their culture as in their constitutions. Canada was an adult community, from 1867 a self-governing 'dominion', culturally and economically influenced by the neighbouring United States. Australasia and Africa embodied several distinct colonies inhabited by both new colonists and settled colonials. India was a heterogeneous empire whose English-speaking subjects consisted partly, in the Victorian sense, of 'Anglo-Indians' with a literate Englishman's taste in reading and partly of Indians and 'Eurasians' with a galloping hunger for western education. The rest of the British possessions fall roughly into these or similar categories. From the point of view of copyright legislation Canada is by far the most important. Anything Canada got away with other oversea territories would be sure to copy.

We have already seen how in the forties legislation at Westminster designed to keep cheap piracies out of Canada was in Gladstone's words 'first evaded and then relaxed'. It was relaxed by the foreign reprints act of 1847 which allowed such colonies as secured the concession to import foreign-printed books which would otherwise have been piratical. An *ad valorem* protective duty not exceeding 15 per cent was to be imposed on such imports, and the proceeds less the cost of collection and transmission were to be applied in compensating the British copyright owner. But the duty proved unenforceable, particularly along Canada's 3,000 miles of open frontier with the United States, so that in practice very little cash reached very few United Kingdom authors and publishers. Before the passing of the 1847 act the third Earl Grey, secretary for the colonies, in a circular letter to colonial governors had encouraged the belief that the imperial government would endorse any local legislation on copyright 'notwithstanding any repugnancy of any such law or ordinance to the copyright law of [the United Kingdom]'. Nothing came of this proposed reversal of a fundamental constitutional tradition. Lord Grey's circular was binding on no one. But like the Balfour declaration on a Jewish national home it was regarded for years to come as a 'promise' shamelessly unfulfilled. To the end of the century and beyond it

Canadian politicians continued to inveigh against Westminster's denial of Canada's 'promised' right to legislate on copyright at her own sweet will.

The British North America act of 1867 which made Canada the empire's first self-governing dominion delegated to the governor-general the function of the crown to assent to enactments of the dominion parliament. The governor-general could however withhold assent to, and 'reserve' for consideration in Westminster, any legislation in conflict with imperial law. The dominion's first copyright act (31 Vict. c. 54) in 1868 was unexceptionable, but the Ottawa parliament immediately fell to debating Canadian grievances—grievances common to others of the Queen's adult or adolescent territories. The House of Lords' judgment in *Routledge* v. *Low* had recently attempted to clarify imperial law regarding colonial copyright. According to this judgment protection granted to a book first published in the United Kingdom extended to all the Queen's dominions, but books first published in a British territory oversea though they might acquire local copyright under a local law, if that law had been approved by order in council, secured no copyright in the United Kingdom or in other oversea territories. In the words of the *Athenaeum*†

The result of this opinion of the House of Lords is very disastrous, and justly creates great dissatisfaction in the Colonies and India; it has either destroyed all copyright property in the numerous works which, since 1842, have been first published there, or rendered such property comparatively worthless; and this hardship is increased by the fact that, since 1842, it has been and still is compulsory upon *all* publishers in the British dominions *gratuitously* to send one copy of every book published by them to the British Museum, and four to the Libraries of Oxford, Cambridge, &c.

The anomaly and injustice of such a state of our copyright law become the more apparent when it is remembered that, under the *International* Copyright Conventions entered into by England with France, and most of the other chief European states, works first published in France, &c. have long been, and may still be, protected from piracy in the United Kingdom or any other part of the British dominions.

† 20 November 1869. The first of the paragraphs quoted was adopted almost verbatim in *Copinger on Copyright*, 1870, and later editions.

The quotation illustrates a grievance of the copyright owner whether author or publisher. The Canadian bookseller's grievance, shared by his customers, was that British books were prohibitively expensive. Three-deckers apart, a London novel priced 6s. would be invoiced at a discount of 25 or 30 per cent, namely at 4s. 6d. or 4s.† At the very most an American edition of the same book would retail at U.S. $1.00 (3s. 7d.) and the Canadian bookseller could retail at Canadian $1.00 (4s. 1¼d.) even in the improbable event of his having paid the protective duty—12½ per cent in Canada—designed to compensate the author. Yet many American piracies, priced at perhaps 35 cents were shoddy goods to which British editions would but for their price have been greatly preferred. (During the winter closing of the St. Lawrence British books could only reach Canada *via* the United States. Unless sent in bond, which the publishers thought troublesome for small consignments, they were subject to United States as well as Canadian import duty. This provided a further incentive to Canadian booksellers to replenish stocks with American piracies.) Canadian publishers believed that they could compete with American imports if they were allowed to print editions in Canada without the copyright owner's express sanction. Moreover the higher wages paid in the United States combined with high taxation resulting from the American civil war would, they argued, more than offset the United States protective tariff and enable Canadian-printed editions to undersell American reprints in the American as well as the Canadian market. In other words the Canadians sought licence to do what their unlicensed American neighbours had long been doing: but they were prepared to pay for the licence. The proposal made in 1869 was that, instead of the unenforceable 12½ per cent protective duty on imported American editions, Canadian publishers should be allowed to reprint United Kingdom copyright works at will on payment of an excise duty of 12½ per cent which would go to the author by way of royalty. This is rather like the twilight period introduced into British copyright law in

† Several British publishers allowed Canadian booksellers a further discount of 10 per cent. In the United States discount was normally 40 per cent.

1911, the period from twenty-five to fifty years after an author's death in which any publisher might reprint a work without authorization on payment of a fixed royalty.

The proposal was clearly repugnant not only to imperial copyright law but to the interest of the United Kingdom publisher whose aim was to capture an expanding colonial market for his own editions. The British publisher also feared lest licensed Canadian books should find their way into the United Kingdom market and undersell copyright British editions. In 1872 a bill† passed by the dominion parliament embodying the fixed royalty principle was reserved by the governor-general but was refused assent in Westminster. After protracted correspondence between the ministry of agriculture in Ottawa and the colonial office and board of trade in Westminster—the board of trade tending to side with the Canadians—another Canadian act (38 Vict. c. 88) was passed in 1875. The fixed royalty proposal was considerably modified (being limited to books which had gone out of print, and requiring a licence from the minister of agriculture) and a distinctive Canadian copyright was established. United Kingdom and other authors could secure this copyright even though their books had previously been published elsewhere in the empire, and they were protected against the import into Canada of American or other unauthorized editions. The act was approved by order in council but only after Westminster had passed the Canada copyright act (38 & 39 Vict. c. 53) which prohibited the unauthorized import into the United Kingdom of Canadian editions.

Canadian publishers quickly proved one of their points. Evidence before the royal commission shewed that within nine months of the Canada copyright act a number of books had been published with authority in Canada at prices appreciably lower than those of unauthorized American reprints. Yet Canada was by no means satisfied. Across the frontier in the late 1880s the United States was moving towards the Chace act with its protectionist requirement that copyright books be manufactured in

† *Parliamentary Papers*, Correspondence between the Colonial Office and the Governments of Canada, &c., pp. 5–7; 1875 (144), li.

the States. Ottawa anticipated this in 1889 with an act (52 Vict. c. 29) requiring manufacture in Canada within one month of publication elsewhere. One effect would have been that any book copyright in Britain (or America) and not immediately reprinted in Canada could after one month be reprinted by any Canadian publisher who thought it profitable. Another possible effect might have been that *all* British books would lose protection in the United States: for the benefits of the Chace act were only extended to Britain on the assurance of Lord Salisbury, prime minister and foreign secretary, that United States authors would obtain the same protection in all parts of the British Empire. However the Canadian act of 1889 though it received the royal assent was abortive: Westminster disapproving, the governor-general did not issue the requisite proclamation naming the day when it should come into force. Accordingly the controversy over Canadian copyright lasted well into the twentieth century. Even after Westminster's imperial copyright act of 1911 (1 & 2 Geo. V, c. 46) which applied to most of the empire apart from the self-governing dominions Canada stood alone. Copyright laws on much the same lines as Westminster's were passed within two years of 1911 in India, Australia, New Zealand and even in the Channel Islands and Papua, all of which adopted the Berlin convention of 1908 (successor to the Berne convention). Canada did not fall into line until 1924, and then only because her government had come belatedly to realize that her laws militated against the interest of her own people.

The late eighties were a time of copyright ferment not only in the new world but in Europe and throughout the British empire. 1885 saw the first draft of the Berne international convention. Several of its provisions conflicted with existing British law. A new international copyright act (49 & 50 Vict. c. 33) was accordingly passed in order to iron out the discrepancies and the opportunity was taken to remove outstanding colonial grievances. Copyright registered in a colony was given validity throughout the empire. Furthermore the oppressive requirement that colonial publications

should be deposited in libraries in the United Kingdom was removed. The relevant section was specific.

8. (1.) (b)—where such work is a book the delivery to any persons or body
of persons of a copy of any such work shall not be required.

One such body of persons, the trustees of the British Museum, was
not happy about this erosion of a long cherished privilege. The
best the museum could hope to do was to claim a copy of any
colonial publication which was sold on the United Kingdom
market, a claim vigorously resisted by colonial agents and wholesalers in Britain. As late as 1909 Mr. Frederic Kenyon, the newly
appointed director and principal librarian of the museum, took the
opinion of the law officers of the crown on this point. Their
answers† provide another illustration of inconsistency between
acts of parliament. To the wider question whether delivery to the
museum was required of a book first published abroad and later
published in the United Kingdom the law officers replied that it
was so required under section 6, still in force, of the imperial act
of 1842. They went on to say that delivery of a colonial publication
was indeed dispensed with under section 8 of the 1886 act but that

the position is thus made somewhat illogical, justifying the surmise that
parliament in passing the act of 1886 did not correctly appreciate the existing
law. But we do not think that is a sufficient reason for not giving effect to
the earlier statute.

So the British Museum won, at least for a time.

We must now return to the seventies, not to the backwoods but
to the outback. To the royal commission Mr. Farrer confessed:

I have been unable to ascertain what is the nature of the book trade in
Australia; whether they buy and read our expensive British editions, or
whether they get cheap American reprints, or whether they reprint for
themselves.

I find myself nearly a hundred years later in much the same state of
ignorance as Mr. Farrer and that in spite of the help I have received

† Law Department, 15 July 1909. Rights of the British Museum, &c., under the
Copyright Act (5 & 6 Vict. cap. 45). Questions, &c., submitted to the Law Officers of the
Crown and Mr. Rowlatt, with their opinion.

and gratefully acknowledge from librarians and others in Melbourne and Adelaide, Wellington and Auckland.

If Canada was the most important of the British oversea possessions from the point of view of copyright law her very independence of spirit made her for a time less important than Australia as a market for publishers in the old country. The 1870s saw a vast expansion of United Kingdom trade with Australasia. Between 1870 and 1876 the value of British books exported to the United States remained more or less constant—it was in fact tending to fall—between £200,000 and £300,000 a year; to Canada book exports increased by some 33 per cent from £53,000 to £70,000. The figures for Australia shew a rise of more than 150 per cent, from something under £130,000 in 1870 to something over £330,000 in 1876. It ought to be possible to determine the reading habits of Australians and New Zealanders from catalogues of libraries and from reviews and advertisements in newspapers. But these sources do not throw much light on publishing activities. Surviving catalogues range from those of local authority libraries in the larger towns to small circulating libraries on remote sheep stations. As the catalogues give little indication, more usually no indication, of editions or dates (and the catalogues themselves are often undated) they are not very helpful. Local newspapers in the principal ports sometimes listed the titles of books received by the latest ship to call: but here again it is not possible except by guesswork to identify publishers or editions or even to determine whether the books were of legitimate British or piratical American origin. (The concession under the foreign reprints act had not been extended to the Australian colonies.) Advertisements can be positively misleading. A list of 'books of last year's publication' may contain titles repeated from a similar list of three or four years earlier.† The greater number of titles advertised or listed in news columns tended to be theological, educational or standard English classics, with little or no up-to-date general literature or fiction.

† This is only an extension on a grand scale of the British publishers' practice, familiar to bibliographers, of advertising a book as 'published this day' in several successive issues of a weekly periodical. Publication day remains undetermined.

From the 1860s onwards and indeed earlier British publishers had exported books to Australia through wholesale houses whose Australian travellers 'travelled' indiscriminately the wares of all the publishers. Once the books had been delivered to the wholesaler in London—the chief of whom was George Robertson & Company of Melbourne, with a London office and branches sooner or later in Sydney, Adelaide, Brisbane and Auckland—the British publisher lost sight of them. This seems to have been the normal procedure throughout the seventies, though as early as 1874 the Glasgow firm of Collins established a bible warehouse and showroom in Sydney, a city of strong Scottish affiliations. Not until 1884 did any London publisher set up a full-scale branch in Melbourne with its own staff of colporteurs. In that year Cassell's took the lead with cheap publications, mainly weekly and monthly serials of a religious, educational or self-educational character. Ward, Lock followed a few months later with a competitive but rather less forbidding list. In 1884–5 one of the younger Macmillans, Maurice, who had been a schoolmaster before he turned publisher, made an extensive tour of the schools and universities of India and Australasia with a view to studying educational needs.† On his return his firm entered into an agreement with Robertson's London agent, a Mr. Petherick, for the distribution of their various educational series and their magazines. One thing Maurice Macmillan almost incidentally discovered was that cultured Australians could not get the recreational reading they wanted. Small town and outback lending libraries held small stocks of not very recent books. Cheap American unauthorized editions were not uncommon—as how should they be when, as a New South Wales official once wrote to Cassell's, 'This Government takes no steps to prevent the importation of American reprints of English books into the colony': Cassell's were advised to seek redress in the courts *after* importation and sale. (There were however instances of cus-

† The history of educational publishing in the empire is a subject for the social historian rather than the bibliographer. The fact that there were probably more piracies of English textbooks in India and the far east than of any other category of publication in any other part of the world is a tribute to the determination of the oriental races to improve themselves—if westernization spells improvement.

toms seizure of cargoes of American bibles, to the indignation of local missionaries though to the satisfaction of the bible-printing societies in Britain.) Recent British novels might appear as local newspaper serials, with or without authority. The newspaper or magazine was the Australian author's most readily accessible forum, but he only obtained Australian and not United Kingdom copyright. An example is Thomas Alexander Browne, police magistrate of Albury, New South Wales: after *Robbery under Arms* (London 1888) had made his fame as 'Rolf Boldrewood' one of his earlier serialized novels was promptly reprinted, legitimately but without his consent, in Britain. Kipling's earliest writings, published in Calcutta and Lahore, were unprotected elsewhere under palm and pine.

'The cry in India', wrote Marion Crawford, who had been a journalist in Allahabad, in 1886, 'is for cheap books, especially among the Eurasians, who read greedily.' 'The complaint in the colonies', Frederick Macmillan wrote to Thomas Hardy in the same year, 'has been that it has been impossible to get good *new* books at a reasonable price. By the time a book has reached a cheap edition in the ordinary course, colonial buyers want something fresher.' This was the impetus behind the first 'colonial library' since John Murray's of forty years earlier. Murray's Colonial and Home Library was as its name implied aimed at a double market: the books—some new, some old—were to be sold at the same cheap price at home as in the colonies. Macmillan's Colonial Library† was specifically designed 'for circulation only in India and the British Colonies'. Like John Murray before them Macmillan's planned to include old as well as new books and for the same reason. They had a number of suitable titles already in their list. Volumes 1 and 2 in the new library for example were Lady Barker's *Station Life in New Zealand* and *A Year's Housekeeping in South Africa*: having purchased the imperial copyright in these a

† It was originally to have been Macmillan's Indian and Colonial Library. At the instigation of Kipling the name was changed in 1913 to the Empire Library for circulation in the Dominions over the Seas and India. Colonial libraries did not survive the first world war.

dozen or more years earlier the publishers had no fee to pay the author. Unlike Murray on the other hand they had no prejudice against fiction: volumes 5–8 were novels by Marion Crawford including one only recently published in London. 'Good *new* books at a reasonable price, . . . something fresher' than a 6*s.* one-volume reprint of a six-months-old three-decker and also cheaper. . . . New novels in cloth or wrappers were to be shipped to the colonies at the earliest date, if possible by the same ship as carried the magazines in which the three-deckers were advertised or reviewed. This ties up naturally with the single-volume editions prepared for publication in the United States at the same time as the London three-decker and well in advance of the London single volume: the same type-setting would serve for all three one-volume editions, American, colonial and United Kingdom.

Both in New York and in the colonies Macmillan's published besides books in their London list others in which they did not hold the United Kingdom rights. In such instances they usually bought plates or sheets from the United Kingdom publisher. But on occasion they would have a book set solely for the colonial library. In its first year they bought the colonial rights in Hardy's *The Mayor of Casterbridge*. Smith, Elder's two-volume edition of this book after a disappointingly small sale was remaindered within nine months and no cheap edition followed in London for some years. I have not collated the text of the colonial *Mayor of Casterbridge* as I have not seen a copy: colonial editions are hard to come by not only in our country but also, Australasian and South African booksellers tell me, in theirs. Inasmuch as Hardy made considerable revisions between his first London and first New York editions, both of 1886, there is at least a possibility that the colonial edition, also of 1886, is textually different from both.

For the distribution of the colonial library Macmillan's made use of George Robertson's London office which was already handling their educational books. Edward Augustus Petherick had joined Robertson's in Melbourne in 1862 at the age of 15. He entered their London branch in 1870 and soon became its manager. In 1887 he left to set up on his own with a capital of £800.

Announcing the establishment of The Colonial Booksellers' Agency in Paternoster Row he described himself as 'a lover of books and, I hope, "a man of business".' The love of books remained with him to the end.† After seven years his business went bankrupt owing £50,000 to the London publishers and the Australian bank which had financed him. To those publishers he claimed to have paid in his meteoric seven years upwards of £180,000 for the purchase of books which he had either handled as a colonial distributor or published over his own imprint. He had also issued a quarterly trade paper, *The Colonial Book Circular and Bibliographical Record* (fig. 11), later titled *The Torch*. In direct competition with Macmillan's colonial library and George Robertson's Australian Series he had started in 1889 Petherick's Collection of Favourite and Approved Authors, of which number 1 was Hardy's *Desperate Remedies* and number 2 Meredith's *Rhoda Fleming*.

At the suggestion of his assistant J. H. Isaacs (later known to bibliography as Temple Scott) Petherick's collection of approved authors was taken over by one of his creditors, George Bell & Sons, the publishers as will be remembered of the colonial edition of *The Amazing Marriage*. Bell's had already found an outlet for their various Bohn libraries through Petherick. They now entered the colonial market in a big way. In 1895 they had three agents in Canada, seven in South Africa, nine in New Zealand and 15 in Australia. By 1901 they had 27 in Canada, 35 in New Zealand and more than 50 each in Australia and Africa, besides others as far flung as Hong Kong, Fiji, Singapore, Port Said and Trinidad. By this time some 15 London publishers besides Bell's and Macmillan's were running colonial libraries. I mention this expansion in the fifteen years after the copyright act of 1886 as a fulfilment of the prophesy of Mr. Secretary Farrer with which I began— namely that English-speaking people were destined to cover a large proportion of the world. Mr. Farrer's corollary was that the

† After his failure Petherick became a cataloguer in Francis Edwards's bookshop before returning to Australia as the first archivist to the federal government. He died in 1917 honoured in his own country then as now as the pioneer of Australian bibliography.

No. 1. Vol. I.]   [September, 1887.

The

Colonial Book Circular

And

Bibliographical Record.

Contents.

COMPILED AND PUBLISHED BY

EDWARD AUGUSTUS PETHERICK

AT THE

Colonial Booksellers' Agency.

33, PATERNOSTER ROW

LONDON.

ANNUAL SUBSCRIPTION (POSTED TO ANY PART OF THE WORLD) SIX SHILLINGS.

FIG. 11

remuneration of English authors should be largely increased and
the price of books much diminished.

When Macmillan's embarked upon their colonial library in 1886
the need for a diminished price was certain but the economic remuneration of the author was problematical. Unlike later comers
in the field Macmillan's, pioneers of the net book agreement, did
not for twenty years to come set a retail price on their colonial
volumes. Such a price could in any case only have been nominal.
The volumes were invoiced to London wholesalers at 2s. in cloth
and 1s. 6d. in wrappers: the retail price in the colonies, which most
other publishers in the nineties gave as 3s. 6d. and 2s. 6d., inevitably
depended on local factors including duty and on the cost of trans-
port. By English standards these were assuredly diminished prices.
But how much did they leave for the publisher to pay his author,
and what indeed was he paying him for? Nominally he was paying
for 'colonial rights'. There are several similarities between these
colonial editions and the Baron Tauchnitz's collection of British
authors. Tauchnitz bought 'continental rights' and sold his volumes
in continental countries whether or not those countries had entered
into conventions with Britain. 'Colonial rights' were slightly less
vague after a uniform imperial copyright had been established: but
even then Canada had her own distinctive copyright and it was
still possible for Australian or other rights to be reserved. As a result
conflicts between claimants to the whole or the part often arose.
The fact is that terms like 'colonial' and 'continental' rights did not
appear as such on the statute book. They were matters of private
contract between author and publisher or between one publisher
and another.

Tauchnitz did not attempt to sell his editions in British territories. There was no law national or international against the
import of these editions for sale in Britain if the holder of the
British copyright approved: but obviously the British publisher
would not authorize the import of 1s. 6d. reprints from the Continent when he was selling his own product at twice or four times,
or in the case of a three-decker seven times, that price. There was

no law prohibiting the sale of a colonial library copy in Britain, but it was an essential part of the contract—to quote one example —between George Meredith and Chapman & Hall† that the sheets the latter sold to Bell's for colonial sale should not appear on the United Kingdom market.

> It is agreed . . .
> That the company shall undertake that each copy sold by Messrs. Bell & Sons shall have printed in a prominent position the words 'Printed for Colonial Circulation only' or words to the same effect.
> That it shall be distinctly agreed between the company and Messrs. Bell & Sons that the copies of the said author's works above named shall be issued for colonial circulation only, and that the company shall, in so far as they are able, by agreement with Messrs. Bell & Sons and otherwise, undertake that the retail sale of the above named copies shall take place in the Colonies only.

Tauchnitz preferred to pay his authors a lump sum for continental copyright until competition compelled him to go over to the royalty system. When Macmillan's started what might be regarded as a kind of colonial Tauchnitz series they also favoured outright purchase. At the start they offered Marion Crawford £40 for the colonial copyright in his new novel and when he counterproposed a royalty Frederick Macmillan replied, 'The scheme is at present in a purely experimental stage, but by the time your next novel is ready we shall be able to tell more accurately what the colonial sale will amount to and what we can afford to do'. In the same year Macmillan's bought Hardy's *The Mayor of Casterbridge* (a Smith, Elder novel) for £25; two years later they paid Hardy £50 for *Wessex Tales* (which they published in London) and— after a little haggling—Mrs. Humphry Ward £75 for *Robert Elsmere* (again Smith, Elder). Among other doubts they could not be certain, whatever they may have told their authors, whether a 2s. 6d. colonial paperback might not prejudice the sale of a domestic 6s. edition. Blackwood's, it will be recalled, had expressed a similar doubt to George Eliot about Tauchnitz reprints in the sixties, and George Eliot only after some hesitation decided in

† 15 November 1894. Texas University Library.

favour of Tauchnitz. Apropos of *The Mayor of Casterbridge* Hardy wrote to Frederick Macmillan that Mr. Smith of Smith, Elder

suggests that I should consider whether such an edition would affect the sale of a cheap English edition I might hereafter publish. Now that is a matter on which you are the best judge. . . . Personally I rather like the idea of this colonial library which you have been so enterprising as to publish. You will probably know from experience of your own cheap editions if the new library has interfered with them at all.

Macmillan's reply was that in his firm's experience the sale of 6s. novels in the colonies had been 'very small indeed' and that with the new library they hoped 'to tap a practically new market'. They did.

The initial editions were not large, usually 500 or 1,000 copies. In 1894 Bell's, who built up their colonial library by purchasing editions in sheets from other publishers, bought six novels by Gissing† and seven by Meredith—1,500 copies of Gissing's latest novel *In the Year of Jubilee* but only 750 of his older novel *The Emancipated*, while the figures for Meredith ranged between 750 and 1,000. By that date yielding to pressure from authors and to competition with a growing number of publishers Macmillan's had become reconciled to paying royalties for colonial rights. (One of their active rivals in the early nineties was William Heinemann whose Colonial Library of Popular Fiction (fig. 12) was as menacing to Macmillan's as his Leipzig-based English Library was in the same period to Tauchnitz.) The standard royalty for all colonial libraries for the next twenty years or so was 4d. a copy. That it was not a straight percentage of the retail price was because there were copies both paper-bound and in cloth. The number of copies put up in either form at any one time would depend on the size of the demand in one or another colony. Fourpence represents

---

† Gissing described this to his friend Eduard Bertz as a sale to 'an Australian firm' and indeed his London publishers Lawrence & Bullen had previously sold sheets of his books to Petherick. The persistence of the idea that the colonial market was largely an Australian market was natural though in fact Petherick had covered most of the empire. Bell's even before Petherick's failure had wide contacts in India and made a point of calling theirs an 'Indian and Colonial' library. They were as anxious to interest the nabobs, remote from Mudie's, as the settlers in the outback.

Heinemann's Colonial Library
of Popular Fiction.

Published for Sale in the British Colonies and India only.

OUIDA	*The Tower of Taddeo*
MARY L. PENDERED	*A Pastoral Played Out*
E. S. PHELPS	*The Master of the Magicians*
Mrs. RIDDELL	*The Head of the Firm*
AMÉLIE RIVES	*According to St. John*
ADELINE SERGEANT	*Out of Due Season*
,,	*The Story of a Penitent Soul*
FLORA ANNIE STEEL	*The Potter's Thumb*
,,	*From the Five Rivers*
R. L. STEVENSON and L. OSBOURNE	*The Ebb Tide*
H. SUTCLIFFE	*The Eleventh Commandment*
TASMA	*A Knight of the White Feather*
W. EDWARDS TIREBUCK	*Miss Grace of All Souls'*
H. G. WELLS	*The Island of Dr. Moreau*
PERCY WHITE	*Mr. Bailey-Martin*
,,	*Corruption*
MARY E. WILKINS	*Jane Field*
H. F. WOOD	*Avenged on Society*
I. ZANGWILL	*The Master*
,,	*Children of the Ghetto*
,,	*The Premier and the Painter*
EMILE ZOLA	*Stories for Ninon*
Z. Z.	*A Drama in Dutch*

THE FOLLOWING WILL BE PUBLISHED DURING 1897.

MAX NORDAU	*The Malady of the Century*	Jan.	6
	Told in the Verandah	,,	20
Z. Z.	*The World and a Man*	,,	27
EMMA BROOKE	*Life the Accuser*	Feb.	10
W. W. JACOBS	*Many Cargoes*	,,	17
W. E. NORRIS	*The Dancer in Yellow*	,,	24
MARTIN J. PRITCHARD	*Without Sin*	Mar.	10
FLORA ANNIE STEEL	*On the Face of the Waters*	,,	17
HECTOR MALOT	*Her Own Folk*	,,	24
HENRY JAMES	*Embarrassments*	,,	31
W. J. LOCKE	*At the Gate of Samaria*	Apl.	7
PERCY WHITE	*Andria*	,,	14
Mrs. ALEXANDER	*Mammon*	,,	21
ROBERT HICHENS	*The Folly of Eustace*	,,	28
I. ZANGWILL	*The King of Schnorrers*	May	19
ADELINE SERGEANT	*The Failure of Sibyl Fletcher*	,,	26
M. HAMILTON	*McLeod of the Camerons*	June	9
HENRY JAMES	*The Other House*	,,	16
ROBERT HICHENS	*Flames*		

London: WM. HEINEMANN, 21, Bedford Street, W.C.

FIG. 12. Colonial Library wrapper 1896

13⅓ per cent on a paper-bound copy retailed at 2s. 6d., and 9½ per cent on a cloth copy at 3s. 6d.; or if one assumes an equal sale in both forms an average royalty of a little over 11 per cent. Meredith's and Gissing's receipts on this basis would have been somewhere between £12 and £25 for each title. However well or badly their editions sold they may be assumed to have received these sums, for when a colonial edition was published by a firm that did not hold the United Kingdom rights the sheets were purchased outright and paid for within three months of delivery. If the publisher of the colonial edition failed to dispose of the whole impression he stood the loss. If however the same firm published both the United Kingdom and the colonial editions the position might become a little complicated. With several of Henry James's novels published by Heinemann's the surplus colonial sheets, in some instances amounting to half the impression, were never bound up for the undiscriminating colonies but appeared years later on the home market. History does not relate whether the author received 10 per cent on 6s. (i.e. 7d.) as stipulated in his contract for his London editions or a mere 4d. a copy.

A run-of-the-mill colonial edition might sell slowly over many years but the life of a successful novel in this form was not normally long. Its very success led its London publisher to issue 2s. cloth, and later 6d. paperback, editions for combined home and colonial circulation. But an outstanding best-seller at home could be expected to be an outstanding best-seller oversea. When, with *David Grieve* Macmillan's paid £7,000 for combined American and Canadian rights (as what would now be called a loss-leader) they agreed to pay 4d. a copy for colonial rights outside Canada, and having now got the measure of the market they printed a first colonial impression of 18,000 copies which they sold within six months. Mrs. Ward netted £300.

The separation of Canadian from other British copyrights is now commonplace: 'not for sale in the U.S.A. or Canada' is a legend frequently found today in for example Penguin paperbacks. The separation owes nothing to the distinctive Canadian copyright created by the act of 1875 but everything to the special relationship between Canada and the United States after the Chace act of 1891. With reciprocal if unequal privilege between the United States and the British Empire the Canadian market was fiercely disputed between British and American publishers, as it has been ever since. If a Canadian publisher or bookseller had a choice of importing sheets from the United States or from Britain he could do better with American sheets largely because he saved the cost of ocean freight. Moreover an American novel, and the argument applies also to books other than fiction, would be advertised in American newspapers and magazines circulating in Canada at one dollar: Canadian booksellers would expect to pay $1.00 less 40 per cent as against 6s. less 30 (or possibly 40) per cent plus freightage. Even a colonial library novel at 3s. 6d. could not compete, and in any case the British author would prefer to receive 15 per cent on American copies sold in Canada at $1.00 rather than 4d. a copy on a colonial library copy sold there. To this extent Smith, Elder's warning to Hardy was justified, as was Mrs. Ward's inclusion of Canadian with American rights.

If a British publisher controlled all rights, British, colonial and American—and this applies especially to publishers like Macmillan's with a full-scale publishing house in the United States— he would naturally prefer to sell his American dollar edition in Canada rather than his 3s. 6d. colonial, and while sales continued he would have even less incentive to export his paper-bound colonial at 2s. 6d. Yet his London wholesalers who bought in bulk for all the colonies continued to send paper-bound editions to Canada in spite of the publisher's protests and thus to undersell the dollar edition which the same publisher was supplying from the United States. On the other hand a London publisher with no United States copyright could successfully undersell American editions in Canada. This led to a spate of new paper-bound American editions of popular books priced competitively at 75 cents or less in the late 1890s. By and large the only winner in this war of British and American publishers should have been the Canadian reader; yet there were in the eighties and nineties not enough of him. From the commercial angle it was not until long after 1901, the *terminus ad quem* of these lectures, that any sort of order was brought into a highly confused situation.

If sometimes these lectures have seemed to stray from their proper province, international copyright law, I would plead that they have held to international and colonial relations in what modern jargon would call 'the publishing sector'. There is enumerative bibliography and there is analytical bibliography and there are publishing history and printing history. These are all elements of what in my opinion should be regarded as a single discipline. A list—a mere list—of the titles that John Murray included in his colonial and home library or Tauchnitz in his British collection or Petherick among his favourite and approved authors; the variations in imposition or paper or prelim-cancellation between British and American editions before or after 1891 or between British and colonial editions; the differences in printing practices in different countries; the effect upon these and upon publishers of the laws of the different countries at different times—all these if examined together rather than as isolated phenomena should help in re-creating the background in which literature has existed. Basically the study of publishing history is no different from the study of other business activities—distilling, say, or banking or the economy of supermarkets: and statute and case law no less than the law of supply and demand are part of the history of all business evolution. But there is a distinction between books on the one hand and gin or bank loans or mass-merchandizing on the other. What may be called the legal, commercial and general aspects of bibliography deserve as much attention as the enumerative and analytical because of the assistance they can give to what I conceive to be the ultimate justification of all bibliographical exercise, the understanding of writers and their texts: just as I believe that the justification of textual criticism, as also of the unfashionable biographical or the 'non-cognitivist' approach to criticism, lies in what it contributes to appreciation and enjoyment of literature.

I have, if I may indulge in a medley of metaphors, scratched the surface of many fields and stuck out my neck in jungles where a

giraffe might fear to tread. Other explorers will make other dis-
coveries and propound other theories. I would give them one piece
of advice—to move quickly. The intricacies of international law
are fully documented even though bibliographers may not have
fully studied the documents. But the documents vital to the historian of nineteenth-century publishing, such as survive, are fast
being destroyed or dispersed. Even since I began to seek material
for these lectures it was announced by an ex-prime minister, the
chancellor of our university, that one of the largest and most important archives of the period, that of Macmillan & Company,
was to be sold piecemeal at auction—a sale 'of a kind to warm the
cockles of American bibliographical hearts'.† No doubt there were
good business reasons: publishing is a business, not a charitable aid
to bibliography. Even the correspondence preserved from the
nineteenth century by our own Clarendon Press was, when I saw
it, in a sorry state of preservation. It would be regrettable if other
Victorian records of the kind were to be allowed to disappear or
to disintegrate. Time for the bibliographer is running out.

† *The Sunday Telegraph*, 27 June 1965. Happily the decision was rescinded, and the
Macmillan archives were sold to the British Museum in the summer of 1967. The
correspondence files of the Macmillan Company of New York had been presented in
1966 to the New York Public Library.

INDEX

PRINTED IN GREAT BRITAIN
AT THE UNIVERSITY PRESS, OXFORD
BY VIVIAN RIDLER
PRINTER TO THE UNIVERSITY